Flying Lessons
The Psychology of Intimacy and Anxiety

by
John A. Snyder

The imagination loves symbols because it recognizes that inner divinity can only find expression in symbolic form. [1]

Real soul presence has humour and irony and no obsessive self-seriousness. [2]

authorHOUSE™

1663 LIBERTY DRIVE, SUITE 200
BLOOMINGTON, INDIANA 47403
(800) 839-8640
WWW.AUTHORHOUSE.COM

First published by AuthorHouse 12/19/05

ISBN: 1-4259-0129-8 (sc)
ISBN: 1-4259-0130-1 (dj)

Library of Congress Control Number: 2005909984

Printed in the United States of America
Bloomington, Indiana

This book is printed on acid-free paper.

Cover Art: "Crane Choreography"
© Beth Kingsley Hawkins, photographer
See: www.hummerlady.com

Table of Contents

Acknowledgements

This writing would not exist without the help and critical discernment of Charlene Breedlove, my editor, who saw "intriguing possibilities" in my proposals when we first met in Ireland. We talked a lot, we fought a little (respectfully) and we laughed, and together we accomplished something quite special.

I am also deeply grateful to Nancy Steffen-Fluhr for enthusiastically supporting my psychological insights, and throughout this sometimes-tortuous writing process, helping me to say what she knew I wanted to say. My thanks go out to all those readers who took the time to read the manuscript and offer helpful suggestions.

When I need to describe my particular practice of psychotherapy, I describe it as eclectic and see it falling in the category of existential-humanistic. I am particularly indebted to Heidegger and Kierkegaard for an understanding of the human predicament, to Jung for an understanding of the human psyche, to Sullivan for an understanding of human relatedness and to O'Donohue for an understanding of the human blessing.

However, my primary teachers have been the thousands of men, women and young people, sometimes called patients, more often clients, who have trusted me and taught me how to be a resource as they move from patterns of relating to themselves and others that are troubled and estranged toward an experiencing of life that is filled with satisfaction, excitement and love. Nor could I possibly know what I know about loving and authentic human relationships without what I have learned from my children.

I acknowledge Carolyn, my respected partner and co-therapist, for the great adventure of our existential relationship, who would say we have been "free associating" for thirty years, and who volunteered for the duration of this writing project to come dangerously close to being a "wife."

Aryeh Maidenbaum, of the New York Center for Jungian Studies, gets acknowledgment for his leadership in workshops that introduced me to the magic of Celtic Ireland. These experiences, over the past few years, moved me from a total immersion in clinical practice to this adventure in writing.

And Brad Darrach: In unfathomable ways, he has had a hand in this writing!

Finally, I acknowledge Lane Wallace who writes about the romance of small planes in *Flying* magazine under a similar heading: "Flying Lessons."

Frontispiece

With great difficulty,
advancing by millimeters each year,
    I carve a road out of the rock.

For millenniums my teeth have wasted and my nails have broken
    to get there, to the other side,
    to the light and the open air.

And now that my hands bleed and my teeth tremble,
    unsure, in a cavity cracked by thirst and dust,
    I pause and contemplate my work:

I have spent the second part of my life
    breaking the stones, drilling the walls, smashing the doors,
    removing the obstacles

I placed between the light and myself
    in the first part of my life.

Octavio Paz [1]

Preface

While vacationing in the Alps some time ago, I attended a French ski school called SnowFun where the instructors taught skiing entirely through imagery. They were the best lessons I ever had. In the Eastern United States and Canada we're fortunate if there is more snow than ice, and I was having difficulty skiing in the unfamiliar deep powder. My instructor watched me fall headfirst a few times, then asked an odd question:

"Have you ever done any diving?"

"Yes," I said, a bit mystified.

"From a diving board?"

"Yes."

"What did you do?"

Attempting to picture it, I responded: "I took two steps, then bounced on the board with my feet together, and off I went."

"Good, that's what I want you to do here, in the snow."

I focused on the image of diving and suddenly began making beautiful turns in the powder! How could something that strange actually work?

Like the instructors at SnowFun, in this book I use imagery as a teaching tool. I begin each chapter by narrating an incident drawn from more than 2000 hours of flying as an instrument-rated private pilot. Then I suggest how you can use the pictures generated from the flying story to discover exciting truths in your own life. These truths have "face validity," as statisticians like to say. They are things we have always known but have forgotten in our headlong rush to accept what others say we should believe. Once we see such truths and embrace them, the results are dramatic and we cannot believe we ever saw life any other way.

Flying Lessons represents the distillation of my thirty-five year practice as a psychologist — thirty-five years of intimate involvement with people who are trying to find their way out of dark depression and crippling relational conflicts. There is a way out. However, this escape requires giving up comfortable ways of thinking and familiar ways of doing things.

Flying Lessons is about freeing ourselves from the heaviness of depression and the sadness of estrangement from others. This book is about finding pleasure in the feeling side of ourselves. It is about finding lightness and freedom and excitement in satisfying closeness and loving intimacy.

Much of my experience as a therapist has been with people in the helping professions, practicing psychologists and others who desire the quality of excitement and intimacy in their own lives that they are enabling others to create. Because far too much in psychology is unnecessarily convoluted and tediously explained and defended, these psychologists, psychiatrists, clinical social workers, marriage and family therapists, and others find these insights you are about to encounter as exceptionally practical and like a breath of fresh air. My confidence in the value of the insights in *Flying Lessons* is enhanced by their successes in implementing these truths in their practices and sharing the exciting results.

So come join me in some flying adventures. During the journey, we will explore together a series of practical psychological insights that will transform your life and energize your relationships with the people you love.

One playful caution before we begin: Although *Flying Lessons* may be instructive for aviators, it is not a manual designed to teach people how to fly an airplane. Similarly, *Flying* Lessons is not another simplistic psychological self-help book. Reading any book, even a good one, is no substitute for psychotherapy if your life is crashing in flames. What the book does try to do is to reframe some basic existential truths, truths that can help all of us learn to love well and live well. It pictures old dilemmas in fresh ways, in the belief that having better pictures to guide us makes it easier to be healthier and happier, and, in short, to have more fun.

Chapter One:
Sheer Terror

The unlived life is not worth examining.

It was not supposed to be a particularly long flight, about two and a half hours from the Eastern Shore of Maryland to Detroit. We were fully loaded with all the usual stuff plus binoculars, cameras, and spotting scopes — three people in a single engine high- performance four-place airplane. Carolyn had given over the copilot seat to Lester, an expert birder and close friend. Lester serves as our personal bird guide on these pilgrimages each May to Point Pelee, Canada, when thousands of songbirds funnel up and cross the Great Lakes at this particular spot on their way North. Their spring migration offers some of the most spectacular bird watching in North America.

Lester is about the only person to whom Carolyn would surrender secondary control. She has completed the Aircraft Owners and Pilots Association's Pinch Hitter Course and is confident that, under ordinary circumstances, she would be able to get this little airplane back on the ground if something happened to me.

The takeoff was normal. We were relaxed, happy to be on our way. The weather was solidly overcast across the Eastern half of the United

1

States, but I wasn't concerned, as no turbulence or icing was forecast at our planned altitude of 8000 feet and I had had many hours of instrument flight time behind me. This sort of flying in a modern, well-equipped small plane has sometimes been described as "hours of boredom, punctuated by moments of sheer terror." With the autopilot set, our path through the gloom cleared for us by air traffic control, and nothing visible in the clouds, we were in that quiet state, completely unaware that we were rushing headlong into one of those moments of sheer terror.

It happened this way. We had just angled across Lake Erie from over Cleveland. I had readjusted my seat and was reviewing the approach plates in preparation for an instrument approach into the Detroit downtown airport. The landing would need to take place in nearly the minimum required visibility. *Suddenly, without warning, we had a total electrical failure.* The entire panel of lights went blank: no sound in our earphones and no outside horizon to align with. I heard my old flying instructor's voice loudly saying: "Aviate, Navigate, Communicate" (always in that order).

So the first thing to do was to keep the wings level. Because I had an artificial horizon, an airspeed indicator, and an altimeter (none of which are dependent on electricity) I could, with great concentration, theoretically keep us flying and not spin out of control. The engine would also keep running, I hoped, since it had its independent magneto-supplied current. I say this to share information; these were not factors from which I was deriving any comfort at the time.

It's amazing how many pictures can quickly go through one's mind when death seems imminent. The week before, I had read an article called "Spatial Disorientation: The Deadly Killer," which detailed the many fatal accidents that happen when a pilot becomes disoriented during an emergency in the clouds. An image flashed in my mind of an experience I had had in a simulator designed to induce vertigo. I had been given the simple task of reaching down to put numbers in a transponder, and I totally lost control of my simulated airplane. Now, concentrating on very small head movements, I busied myself trying to keep at bay all thoughts of fatal accidents and to manage this predicament.

In these first seconds of panic, I was doing what I could to Aviate (keep the wings level and the altitude constant) and to Navigate ("in times of radio failure, continue to fly the last assigned heading and altitude").

It was time to attempt to Communicate. I tried to reach behind for the backup hand-held transceiver (radio) I keep in the armrest without waking Carolyn. I discovered she was not sleeping. She was thinking, "This is the end, but I have had a very good life," she later reported. All I saw at the time was her face buried in the pillow she clutched to her breast.

Communicating through a little hand-held radio is not easy at best and can be disorienting in a loud cockpit. I could not believe how LOUD it was. Nonetheless I was able to establish contact with Air Traffic Control, declare an emergency and state our problem. The standard phraseology ATC uses in such a situation is marvelous: "Zero Foxtrot Quebec (our call sign), what are your intentions?" I mean, cut me a break! What are my intentions? It was hard not to reply in dead earnest: "My intentions? Hopefully somehow to live!"

Trying to sound calm, and doing the best I could to lower my tone several octaves; I replied that I would like to have vectors (directions) to the nearest VFR airport (one with good visibility under the clouds). ATC: "State available fuel." The fuel gauges are electric in my plane, but I had been trained to keep track by time, so I knew I had about an hour and a half left, which I reported. There was a long pause on the other end. Then a second moment of terror: "Zero Foxtrot Quebec, there are no VFR airports within your range. Low ceilings and limited visibility are very widespread, with most airports reporting one mile or less visibility and ceilings of five to six hundred feet. Say intentions."

There's that word again! I decided to give my intentions some thought this time, but I was not feeling very hopeful of survival for my friends and myself. The best I could come up with was: "I would like a climb to a level that would put me between cloud layers to reduce my workload, and then I would like vectors to the nearest military base that might have PAR capability (a more precise guidance to a runway)."

Once given permission to climb, I was able to find a narrow area between cloud layers and turn to our newly assigned heading. Then it was time to trouble-shoot. The first thing to do is to reset the master breaker switch, I reminded myself. If it pops off, turn everything off (many, many switches) and then turn them on one by one in an attempt to identify the culprit. Surprise, surprise, the lights come on, and the breaker holds. At first, I was afraid of being thrust into darkness again, but after five or ten minutes it seemed best to ask for vectors back to downtown Detroit for landing, at an airport I was very familiar with. Needless to say, on the ground in Detroit that evening there were three very grateful human beings whose legs were too weak to walk.

At this point, you might ask, "Why did you put yourself in such a potentially dangerous situation in the first place? Do you have some screws loose?" For a practicing psychologist, who has spent many hours and much money being analyzed, that would be a rather embarrassing answer. So let me offer an alternative explanation. The philosophical basis of my psychotherapy practice is existentialism. Don't worry. I am *not* going to launch into a discussion of what existentialism means, except to say that existentialism starts from experiential knowledge rather than from abstract systems or *a priori* assumptions. This experiential knowledge tells us that feeling anxious is inseparable from being human and being alive.

Unfortunately, these days anxiety is generally used to designate a pathological state, that is, to define an illness. We are bombarded with advertisements for drugs promising to cure us of just such an illness. Of the psychopharmacological drugs available, many are probably efficacious; however, they can have disturbing side affects. More importantly, these drugs are often unnecessary.

What is anxiety? Anxiety is the experience of feeling out of control and vulnerable, aware that something untoward could happen. That's it!

But what does that really mean? In our unconscious, and particularly in our collective unconscious, it means a great deal. Let's assume for a moment that we do not begin when we are born; rather, that going back through our parents, grandparents, great grandparents, and so on, we carry some deep-seated feeling memory of the struggle of our evolution from amoeba to human being. Psychologist Carl Jung believed that in addition to our immediate consciousness, which is of a thoroughly personal nature, there exists a second psychic system of a collective, universal, and impersonal nature, a memory of where we come from in our evolution to the human beings we are today. The unconscious, Jung believed, thinks and behaves in terms of thousands of years. [1]

Again, anxiety is the experience of being out of control and vulnerable, aware that something dire could happen. Our collective unconscious signals that we are about to be eaten or are in some other way being exposed to the threat of psychic annihilation. It is understandable that our reaction is to do whatever we can do to avoid such an experience. But, ah, here is the rub: Avoiding anxiety is probably one of the worst choices we can make with our lives.

I am reminded of a time recently when I needed to retrieve my boat from the back of a boatyard after a flood. Great piles of debris lay haphazardly on the ground, and as I was beginning to thread my way through, Dick (who worked there) shouted: "Doc, be careful back there; there are snakes around." Then he added, "Now none of these snakes we have around here will hurt you; but they will surely make you hurt yourself!" Anxiety is a little like that. Feeling anxious and vulnerable won't really hurt us. But avoiding anxiety can do us real harm.

Anxiety cannot be eliminated; it belongs to our human existence. Every time we choose to avoid anxiety, we die a little in the midst of life. Moreover, every time we choose to avoid anxiety, we make it more difficult in the future to choose anything that could conceivably make us anxious. The result is that we withdraw more and more from whatever would enable us to feel alive and vital and excited. In other words, we move toward depression and death. Neurosis, said theologian Paul Tillich, is an attempt to avoid nonbeing by avoiding being itself. [2] In other words, we die to keep from dying.

It is possible that one could freeze with fear or anxiety. Stage fright could result in not being able to speak one's lines. That is the bad news. The good news is one does not stay frozen. Anxiety can be embarrassing, but it is not deadly.

Again, to be alive is to be anxious. The existentialists are correct when they remind us that we are not in control of our destiny. We are vulnerable. We are not secure. We are not safe. We all will die eventually and could die any minute. The anxiety of not being able to preserve one's own being underlies every fear. To live exciting lives, to experience any growth or change, to move into any intimacy with another human being, we have to embrace this very real existential anxiety.

Recently I heard from a former client who called to share her current life and work. She said, "I'm sure you will be pleased; I'm scaring myself a lot. I remember how I used to be so careful, so withdrawn from life, none of the energy I feel today. I talk to everyone with whom I work about how important it is to live life scaring ourselves, making ourselves anxious."

He dreamed about bears and called it a nightmare. He was in the woods where bears often prowled, and he was extremely anxious, waking up in a cold sweat. Jim was in his mid-thirties and had suffered from a low-grade chronic depression most of his life. He experienced a host of feelings so unacceptable to him that he used most of the energy needed for living to keep these feelings at bay. He had accepted his low libido, lack of energy and excitement, and all the other symptoms of depression as normal. One of the symptoms — minimal sexual interest — was partly responsible for the dissolution of his marriage. Being a practicing psychologist, he realized he needed to seek help in understanding what part he might have played in his failed marriage.

We had focused for some time on ways Jim could take more risks and make his life more exciting. He understood that he needed to make a change and not always seek safety and security. He had started talking more openly with his friends about what he was feeling and even frightened himself by confronting one friend about the hurt and abandonment he had felt when the friend had left him alone in a bar when some drunken men had begun to fight.

But what had really made Jim anxious was that he had met a woman — a lively, sexually forthright woman, toward whom he felt a strong attraction, an attraction that she also felt. He liked who she was as a person, and they talked for hours, discovering many mutual interests. One thing led to another, and she ended up spending the night with him — the night he had the nightmare about the bears.

I was curious as to whether he had ever had a dream like this before. He responded: "Oh, yes, many times. I used to have this dream a lot.

Then they stopped a long time ago." In my devilish way, I said: "That's too bad. I mean it's too bad that they stopped." This, of course, got Jim's undivided attention. We explored what had been happening in his life when the bear dreams ceased and discovered together that it had been a time of serious, heavy repression of his feelings. His recognition of the bear dream as a sign that he was scaring himself and moving out of his depression became a turning point in Jim's life.

Often it is difficult to find people who will support us in embracing anxiety. Our risk taking can make others anxious, and the result can be bad advice. Jim had one friend who was adamant that he see the nightmare as a warning sign. Even some therapists might have seen dreaming of bears as a sign of something foreboding. Therapists, too, must live by embracing anxiety if they wish to support clients in making healthy life-affirming choices.

The good news is that when we make a choice that involves some anxiety, it becomes easier to make other anxiety-laden choices. In that way, we open our lives to ever more aliveness and excitement.

The bottom line: *Every choice we make is either a movement toward anxiety and excitement or a movement toward depression* — sometimes with minor consequences, sometimes with major consequences. The aliveness and vitality that accompany risk-taking support healthy immune functioning and contribute to well-being. The heaviness and lethargy that accompany risk avoidance diminish immune functioning and become the seedbed for much physical illness.

Clearly, not everyone should take up small-plane flying, soar into the clouds, and have a complete electrical failure. However, it is clear to me that such an experience leads to a renewed commitment to live authentically, without dissembling and with heightened capacity to celebrate every minute the beauty and privilege of being alive.

Sometimes, it seems, we really have no other choice but to leap into anxiety. A dream, often retold and one I attribute to Jung, vividly illustrates the choice between depression and anxiety. In this dream Jung found himself in a cave-like barren place, traveling down a fairly well-marked passageway. He had not gone far before he came to a dark and foreboding opening that seemed to invite him into the void. He hurried past it, looking for a way out, only to find himself increasingly frantic as he circled back to that same scary opening. Thinking he had not looked hard enough for an escape route, he searched again along each wall. Still he came back to the awful opening. Maybe, he thought, a passage is hidden in the ceiling, and he explored that. In desperation, he examined the floor. Beginning to panic, he paused longer at the dark opening and finally came to the only possible solution. Summoning all the courage he could, he jumped into the abyss.

Taking on anxiety is like that — a leap into the abyss. Sometimes the only other choice is a circular wandering in an all too familiar and depressive denial of life.

One of the most neglected areas of our life experience, in which anxiety plays a major role, is the choice to relate intimately to others. Without a certain degree of anxiety, we will not be able to sustain the closeness we desire. The vulnerability and exposure we experience in being truly open to another can generate more anxiety than we find bearable. We need courage to leap into the abyss, rather than wander in circular patterns of distant and superficial relating.

As human beings we long for intimacy. As human beings we also like to avoid anxiety — that frightening and seductive place of the abyss. Thus, since anxiety is a concomitant to all authentic human relating, we face a choice.

In close relationships it is tempting to play it safe, avoid conflict and keep much to ourselves. Such accommodation, however, not only makes the relationship dull and predictable; it also creates distance and estrangement. Existentialists like to contrast this kind of shallow, superficial relating with a way of being with others that has a dimension of both excitement and profundity. Habitually avoiding anxiety can lead to utter boredom, which is a form of depression. We know this intuitively and laugh at the joke in which a teacher asks: "Now what is that word for a long-term committed relationship between a man and a woman?" The student quickly responds: "Oh, that's monotony — I mean, monogamy."

To keep a relationship alive, vital, and keen with anticipation, we need to keep scaring ourselves and talk openly about what we are thinking and feeling.

Joe had gotten himself into a dilemma. He had found a way of satisfying some of his sexual curiosity by going on the Internet. The crisis occurred when Mary discovered a suspicious credit card charge. Because Joe felt deeply ashamed and because he truly cared about what Mary was feeling, he promised not to continue exploring these Internet sex sites.

Not surprisingly, this did not solve their problem. Mary could not get it out of her mind when they were making love that Joe was fantasying about other women while relating to her, but she was afraid to talk about that. What she did instead was to avoid all possible intimate interactions. Joe considered her distancing herself to be a punishment for his transgression. At the time he sought help, they had not made love for more than six months. He perceived Mary as extremely angry and attacking most of the time; and he, in his passive-aggressive way, had withdrawn.

It does not take a trained observer to know that these two people needed to be talking. But to talk meant becoming vulnerable, not feeling in control, and fearing something untoward could happen — in a word, anxiety. To not talk is safe, but it creates enormous estrangement and distance. There seems to be no end to how much estrangement we human beings are willing to tolerate to avoid anxiety.

Because the images we have of others largely determine how we actually experience them, much of effective psychotherapy is about helping people change their images. If we hold to images of ourselves interacting in an attacking-defending mode, we might well conclude it would be foolhardy to expect our feelings to matter. We open surprising possibilities when we reveal our vulnerability and anticipate a sensitive, caring response.

A therapist can help by introducing such a picture. For Joe, my suggestion was to change his image of Mary as a frightening woman who would attack him to the image of a woman threatened but perfectly able to care about what he felt. Because it was what he genuinely felt, I urged Joe to go to Mary in a loving way, put his arms around her, and say softly, "Mary, I have been feeling an incredible desire for you; I miss you terribly, and I know we need to talk."

It was clear to Joe that this approach meant taking on more anxiety than he was accustomed to in his relationship with Mary, but he left the session determined to be brave. In the next session Joe arrived despondent saying, "I thought about doing what we talked about; I just couldn't do it."

Harry Stack Sullivan [3] had a way of talking about how we relate to self — our ego — as being divided between a "good me" (the side we show to others as much as possible) and a "bad me" (the side we keep to ourselves as much as possible). Sullivan saw psychotherapy as a process of diminishing the bad me and enhancing the good me. Sullivan was also wise enough to recognize that there was another disintegrated aspect of ourselves: the NOT me. The "not" me includes the ways we can picture being but find so unacceptable that we deny such experiences could be a part of ourselves. The more we define as "not me," the smaller we became as human beings. The more we can accept the "not me," the larger and more complete we become as human beings. (Perhaps psychologists are "expanders" not "shrinks.")

An amazing transformation occurred within Joe when he heard himself saying it was "not me" to do something as anxiety-laden as talking to Mary about what had become a sexual crisis in their marriage. His affect showed a confident determination. "If you talk to Mary you will not have to take up sky-diving," I said. Joe gave me a curious look, and I added that I was contemplating making that my next recommendation. I encouraged him to picture going out on a Saturday morning, taking off in an airplane, and jumping out at 14,000 feet. "Perhaps if you did that, you would not have trouble talking to Mary Saturday night." He laughed.

Somehow we know this truth: The more anxiety we take on, the easier it is to take on more anxiety. The more anxiety we avoid, the more energy we must expend to avoid anxiety. Choosing to play it safe, we deplete our life energy (libido) and choose to depress ourselves.

Or we have "panic attacks." What a strange way to think about ourselves. It is as if we were walking along in a blissful state and suddenly were molested by killer bees. Of course the advertisements promise a quick fix — the killer-bee-destroying pill. A better way to think about and deal with so-called panic attacks is to place the experience within an existential understanding of anxiety.

Susan was referred because she "suffered from panic attacks." She was discouraged about finding a cure, having paid many visits to a clinic specializing in treating people with this "serious pathological disorder" and having tried several pharmacological treatments. She spoke as if she felt doomed to a life of confinement to her house, her safe bedroom.

When I said, without any heaviness of tone, "it sounds as if you sometimes get extremely anxious," Susan responded, "No kidding!" "Right! And I suppose you must be feeling scared and vulnerable and picture some really bad things may happen." Susan, wide-eyed, "Of course!" (with a tone of "how could you be so dumb to ask?"). Feeling confident in a different approach from her previous experiences I asked, "why don't you tell me some of the bad things you picture might happen to you." That opened a floodgate of images, the most intense being, "I see myself somewhere alone and in panic and no one around." "It sounds as if you've had some experiences like that." "Oh, yes, a lot when I was little." We had a lot to talk about over the next few months.

Two matters of importance are illustrated in this example. First, anxiety is a normal human experience of vulnerability accompanied by an awareness that something terrible could happen. There is no "patient." There is no "sickness." Secondly, exploring the images associated with anxiety can be amazingly productive. The feelings that "come up" are often the ones severely repressed and denied expression. When the feelings associated with anxiety are shared within a relationship that is compassionate and understanding, they lose their power to restrict our lives. Interestingly, in every case I observed in which someone was having supposed "panic attacks," the underlying feelings involved buried experiences of isolation and estrangement.

I'm not trying to introduce a new psychological theory here. I am merely observing that how we conceptualize a problem matters. People who believe they have a sickness called "panic attacks" can come to see themselves as passive victims of some impersonal force and miss the crucial connection to the quite normal (in the sense of humanly understandable) experiences that are creating the anxiety.

Interestingly enough, this existential anxiety has sister feelings of fear and excitement. The existentialists say anxiety has a tendency to regress toward fear — fancy language for saying we would much rather be afraid than be anxious. Fear, as opposed to anxiety, has a definite object, something that can be faced, analyzed, combated, or even endured. Anxiety is vague undifferentiated fear; something untoward could happen, but it is difficult to focus on the threat. Many times when we are anxious, we manufacture something to be afraid of. This process can be quite delusional, crazy in fact.

Barry is in a relationship that has become increasingly intense. He recognizes Marcia to be the woman he has been searching for, the person who has long been missing in his life. Yet he is in distress, unable to sleep, unable to paint (he is an artist) — classic symptoms of anxiety. Since, as the poet and scholar John O'Donohue [4] might say, he experiences Marcia with "an ancient recognition of belonging," he is feeling intensely vulnerable: something dreadful could happen and he could lose her.

What does Barry do? He becomes afraid, afraid that she will "cheat on him," be sexually intimate with other men. He has converted his essential human anxiety into a focused fear. He becomes obsessed and begins extracting promises of fidelity, first in general, then in regard to specific scenarios. Understandably, Marcia becomes increasingly irritated with his lack of trust. It gets worse. Barry becomes unbearably controlling, grilling her about where she goes, how she spends her time, whom she sees. "Did you sleep with him?" "Why did you wear *that* skirt?" "Who were you with last evening when I called?" Barry's irrational controlling behavior will predictably have at least one result — it will end the anxiety-laden relationship.

How sad it is that we have so many ways of diminishing the exciting possibilities of life by avoiding anxiety, in this case by turning the anxiety into a crazy, controlling fear.

If there is a tiger directly in our path, we are afraid. If we don't see a tiger but are in an area where tigers might be, we are anxious. To be in an area where we might see a tiger in the wild, while having a reasonable escape route, is exciting. It seems quite probable if we were to use sophisticated imaging technology to measure the mental responses to each of these scenarios we would see the same pattern activated whether we are afraid, anxious or excited.

Basically, what we say we are feeling depends on how we conceptualize or orient ourselves to a given experience.

Irene reported that she was having difficulty experiencing orgasms. Her relationship with Frank was in most other ways quite satisfying to them both. She described coming to a point in their sexual relating when her experience of anxiety would become disorienting: "Everything at that point goes to hell and Frank and I end up completely frustrated and miserably unhappy." I suggested this problem might be related to other issues we had been addressing such as when Irene would experience intense anxiety whenever she began to feel any loss of control. "When you are experiencing this intensity of feeling with Frank, instead of orienting to it as anxiety-laden, why not think of yourself as being very excited?" Certainly this was not a new concept in our work together.

In her next session she came in smiling, exclaiming: "It worked! Although I had to talk to myself over and over about how exciting it was to be this much out of control. (Frowning) But we now have an awful problem." Yes? (Smiling) "We have a terrible time being able to get anything accomplished!"

This vignette by itself would appear to treat a serious problem superficially and perhaps insensitively. However, reorienting oneself to anxiety in this way is far from easy and requires surrendering to an entirely new paradigm.

Since anxiety means feeling out of control and vulnerable, the new picture is that the potential pleasures are worth the risk. Getting "carried away" could be exciting and perhaps nothing dire will happen. After all, it is rather difficult to have a controlled orgasm.

As a practicing psychotherapist I can attest to the fact that it does make a difference in our experiencing of ourselves if we can embrace the anxiety as excitement. Experiencing anxiety in sexual relating is not uncommon, and the problematic sexual experience is transformed into something exciting when conflicted clients can achieve this simple but dramatic reorientation

Viewing excitement as *embraced* anxiety can open up other "exciting" possibilities. In Pascagoula, Mississippi, on a Saturday afternoon, I was checking on the plane at the same time a group of skydivers were circling in preparation for the feather-like stand-up landings they would make on their selected spot. I walked down to join a group of women at a picnic table who had jumped earlier that day — an accountant, Jane; a computer programmer, Judy; a social worker, Janet; and Jennifer who volunteered, "I'm just a housewife." Janet interjected, "she lies, she just quit her job because she and Jim want to have a baby."

When the opportunity arose, I asked, "How is it that you seem so willing to invite this much anxiety into your lives?" Because the question elicited only blank stares, I had to ask more questions. "When are you most anxious, when you stand at that open door at 14,000 feet and look down at all that open sky and the earth far below?" Judy: "Gosh, no! If I am in line I can hardly wait to jump, I am so excited."

Seeing some men and women with chutes on their backs mulling around the plane ready to board for the next jump, I asked, "maybe it's like the jumpers there; when you're walking around on the good solid earth and still have a choice not to go, then you feel the most anxious?"

Jane, "what and miss the thrill of free falling in the air? Not on your life!"

"Well, I was watching those guys in the hanger packing their chutes; surely that must make you anxious," I said. "Suppose you did something wrong and the chute didn't open." Janet, "I'm not anxious about that, I'm just careful." "I'll tell you when I'm anxious," Jennifer interjected. There was a pause, as everyone at the table absorbed her seriousness. "I was incredibly anxious last Sunday evening when I was curled up on the sofa next to Ted with my feet up and the cat purring in my lap and I *thought* about doing this today."

There's an important truth here: The most intense experience of anxiety is likely to be in the contemplation of the risk. Once we accept the inherent anxiety and make the choice, the experience becomes exciting. Excitement is the result of anxiety we have taken on or embraced.

To live exciting, vital lives requires us to embrace anxiety. To use our precious life energy in avoiding anxiety is self-destructive. The inevitable result is an unlived life — a life not worth examining.

People who are not risk-adverse and live open, creative lives don't generally say that life is anxiety-laden; they are more likely to say that life is exciting. To be alive is to be anxious, and anxiety is the concomitant to all growth, vitality, and authentic relating, not a sickness to be treated or an experience to be habitually avoided.

"In the eyes of the world," wrote Kierkegaard, "it is dangerous to venture. And why? Because one may lose….And yet, by not venturing, it is so dreadfully easy to lose that which it would be difficult to lose in even the most venturesome venture — one's self. For if I have ventured amiss — very well, then life helps me by its punishment. But if I have not ventured at all — who then helps me when I lose my self?" [5]

Chapter Two:
Lost Horizons

The unexamined life is not worth living.

"File to Annapolis." That seemed like a strange thing for my instructor, Kevin, to say. With some thirty-five or so hours of flight instruction, I was beginning to see light at the end of the tunnel: a coveted license to fly. From our home base, Annapolis would be directly across the Chesapeake Bay, a short and easy flight. "Call Flight Service and check the weather." Again, my instructor's emphasis seemed a bit strange. Anyone could see it was a clear, albeit hazy, typical August evening in the Eastern United States. During these months of training, I kept an eye to the sky and knew there were no major weather systems anywhere near.

Having done what I was told, I reported to Kevin: "It's VFR (Visual Flight Rules)." That means that fliers with Private Pilot licenses are limited to reasonable visibility: no flying inside clouds. After hiking over to the main terminal to call Flight Service, my tone might have contained a little irritability: "Yes, Kevin, it is VFR" (thinking, any fool can see that — it's a clear summer evening with not a cloud in sight).

"Then, file to Annapolis." So, off we went. Feeling relaxed, I enjoyed the experience of the wheels slipping free of the pavement and savored the freedom of flight. In retrospect, however, I believe I was beginning to feel uneasy before we cleared the last island and headed out over the Bay. Soon I became extremely uncomfortable. Feeling my hands gripping more tightly on the yoke, I said to Kevin: "I'm having a little trouble here. I can't tell much difference between sky and water." Kevin replied with a bit of an edge, "You cannot tell the difference between sky and water?" My first thought was that I had not had my eyes checked in a while, but then I focused with more intense concentration, thinking this was some new test that I needed to pass. By that time I was completely covered in a cold sweat. I fairly screamed, "Kevin, I've lost the horizon." "John, you can't see the horizon?" he asked sternly, as if I were a blind fool. I took a momentary sidelong glance toward Kevin and saw he was grinning. "OK, John, it's my airplane."

"It's my airplane" is a code worked out early in flight training. It means immediately get your feet off the rudder pedals, get your hand off the yoke, and do not touch a thing. Now that I was disabled, Kevin, by reference to instruments, turned us back to the airport, landed, and we went for our debriefing. A very simple, to the point debriefing: "John, I just wanted you to know that VFR over water in the summertime around here doesn't mean a thing, and thinking that way is a good way to get yourself killed."

I thought about that lesson later when I heard about the tragic accident of JFK, Jr. It appears that, while following all the rules, he inadvertently stumbled into a similar situation. There was no one to say, "It's my airplane," and the world continues to mourn the loss of John and Carolyn and Lauren, three young gifted and promising human beings.

When we lose our horizon in life, when we lose that reference point and do not know if we are up, down, or sideways, it is nice to have someone beside us whom we implicitly trust and to whom we can momentarily relinquish control. This is not a bad picture of some forms of psychotherapy.

Mostly, though, what we need to know is that there are disorienting possibilities in life when we have no horizon, no point of reference, and we can get into some very real trouble. Flying an airplane in such disorientation, we are warned about introducing too many control inputs. Macho management clearly will not work. Almost any control inputs can induce vertigo. Without any sense of where we are, we can make a diving turn to the left, overcompensate with a climbing turn to the right, stall the wing and flip ourselves into a graveyard spin. That appears to have been what happened with JFK, Jr. And what happened to him can happen to any of us.

Feelings about being out of control are linked to the issue of dependency. When do we acknowledge our limitations? I have seen many men, and recently more women, get themselves in as much trouble as a disoriented pilot by taking a counter-phobic stance toward dependency. Instead of recognizing their disorientation and helplessness, they react with frantic and erratic attempts at control.

A major insight of Carl Jung, fundamental to the founders of the AA program, was the importance of giving up supposed control over the addiction and surrendering to a higher power. For Jung sometimes that higher power could be the unconscious, our "objective psyche." Some in the AA program shorten this principle to "letting go and letting God." For many people that saying has profound religious implications. It certainly has everyday life implications.

Something richly symbolic resonates when a person says, "I am John Snyder and I am an alcoholic. Once I experience the disorienting affects of alcohol and lose my horizon, my control inputs are so erratic that I spin and crash." Fortunately, I have never had a problem with alcohol, but I have been to AA meetings with clients and friends, and have no trouble identifying with them.

This is not a sales pitch for AA. Major problems can occur when dependency on alcohol shifts to dependency on AA and there is no movement beyond it. The same dependency without resolution can happen in psychotherapy, especially if the therapist has a strong need to nurture and is unaware of that need.

The point is that in our competitive macho culture we easily become over- managing and, because we can seemingly control so much, we seduce ourselves into believing we can control everything. With such an underlying attitude, we can easily fly into a situation where we cannot tell sky from water.

Frequently this happens when people, without prior warning, lose their jobs. Or it can happen when a young person experiences the huge hurtful ending of a love affair. It invariably happens when a mother or father loses a child. These losses are profoundly disorienting. Even without such crises, we are quite adept at causing disorienting emotional conflict and pain in our relationships. Sometimes this disorientation is unconsciously sought. "There is a strange paradox in the soul," writes O'Donohue, "if you try to avoid or remove the awkward quality, it will pursue you." [1] For example, if we say to ourselves, "I can't stand feeling helpless," and we are doing everything possible to keep from feeling helpless, unconsciously we will probably set ourselves up for many helpless-feeling experiences. Such is the nature of our psychic economy.

That the psyche works this way is not a bad thing. All feelings are transitory: they come and they go. Yet, it is sometimes hard to believe that if we just allow feelings of helplessness to overwhelm us for a time, they will pass. Disallowed feelings that have built up over time can threaten to overpower us. An exclamation I commonly hear is: "If I let myself feel that painfully hurt, unbearably sad, or hopelessly abandoned, I would simply drown."

In times of emotional disorientation, another flying image might be helpful. If the airplane is properly trimmed and the pilot encounters sudden turbulence (from weather or the wake of another airplane), the pilot needs to let go of everything — take his feet off the pedals and take his hand off the yoke or "wheel." No matter what unusual attitude the plane has been thrown into, properly trimmed, it will right itself and come back to straight and level flight. What a wonderful picture of letting go, and what a wonderful picture for life!

Another useful flying analogy involves a plane's Attitude Indicator. In the training flight over the Chesapeake Bay with Kevin, I had an attitude indicator (AI in aviation parlance), called by WWII pilots an "artificial horizon." At the time I was not trained in its use. Like a Mandala, an attitude indicator is a device for picturing the wholeness of two halves of a thing. A circle with a center point, the AI is split by a moving diagonal into a brown and a blue side. If the brown side is down and the blue side up and the two are balanced and level, the plane is in straight and level flight. If blue predominates, you are headed into the wild blue yonder. If brown dominates, you are headed straight for mother earth. If the AI is too far askew, it will let the pilot know he is banking too far to the right or too far to the left. When there is limited outside visibility, failure of this one instrument can be the most frightening thing that can happen to a pilot. Loss of a plane's attitude indicator has led to many fatal crashes.

I believe that every one of us comes equipped with an attitude indicator. In a sense, psychotherapy simply calls attention to the presence of an attitude indicator and provides instruction in its use. Being truly healthy and whole means acknowledging all of ourselves, embracing both our brown side and our blue side, our yin and our yang, our Anima and our Animus, the aspects of ourselves that are feminine and the aspects of ourselves that are masculine, the right-hemispheric side and the left-hemispheric side of our brains.

I call this internal attitude indicator a Mandala because, like the most ancient of symbols, it is a circle, containing seemingly contradictory opposites. You may have seen such a circle with curving black and white sides, each containing a shape of the opposite "color," depicting the iteration of yin and yang. Jung was fascinated by the Mandala and used it to describe wholeness in personality formation or personality types. There is "an obvious means by which consciousness obtains its orientation to experience. *Sensation* (i.e. sense-perception) tells you that something exists; *thinking* tells you what it is; *feeling* tells you whether it is agreeable or not; and *intuition* tells you whence it comes and where it is going." [2] It is through embracing these varieties of experience that we become healthy and whole.

"I had always been impressed by the fact," writes Jung, "that there are a surprising number of individuals who never use their minds if they can avoid it, and an equal number who do use their minds, but in an amazingly stupid way. I was also surprised to find many intelligent and wide-awake people who lived (as far as one could make out) as if they had never learned to use their sense organs: They did not see the things before their eyes, hear the words sounding in their ears, or notice the things they touched or tasted. Some lived without being aware of the state of their own bodies." [3]

We have an internal attitude indicator; a perfect split circle or Mandala, that tells us everything we need to know about experiencing wholeness. Oversimplifying more than some Jungian scholars would, I have found it of great practical help to assume we all have a "feminine" side and a "masculine" side. The masculine side manages us, manages others, gets things done, structures and builds things, is organized and disciplined. The feminine side of ourselves enjoys life in the present, relates to the external world through the senses, is intuitive and creative, likes to listen to music, absorb the beauty of a painting, savor a piece of chocolate. The masculine side of ourselves puts out. The feminine side takes in.

In our current culture, women have made gains in achieving wholeness by embracing their "masculine" side, developing the productive, managing competitive aspects of themselves while staying in touch with their feeling, intuitive side. However, most men have not made similar gains in supporting their "feminine" side. Indeed, the idea that men might have a feminine side is still so discomforting that the concept is mostly treated as a joke. "In Western Society," says the psychologist Jean Baker Miller, "men are encouraged to dread, abhor or deny feeling vulnerable or helpless, while women are somehow encouraged to cultivate this state of being. Our cultural tradition unrealistically expects men to discard rather than acknowledge this feeling side that is common and inevitable to us all."[4]

Fear of effeminacy and softness still rules, as does fear of losing one's "essential" masculinity. There is still too much banging and bombing and thrusting, too little taking in of suffering, too little use of intuition and creativity in seeking solutions to interpersonal and international problems. The attitude indicator is displaying far too much brown, too little blue. That is not to deny that some women lean too far into the blue by being too soft, absorbing too much, even inviting abuse. A lack of assertiveness in confronting unfair treatment is an example of unbalanced anima, a lack of "male" soulfulness.

Unfortunately, women who are more assertive are often viewed as deviant. From a male-dominant point of view, these women are not behaving the way women should, not accepting their appropriate role as passive and supportive wives and mothers, for instance. Understandably, women rebel against such narrow stereotyping of human beingness. Judith Butler, a humanistic philosopher, believes the appropriate way to understand gender is as performance. "Taking on gender is not possible at a moment's notice, but is a subtle and strategic project, laborious and for the most part covert. Becoming a gender is an impulsive yet mindful process of interpreting a cultural reality laden with sanctions, taboos, and prescriptions."[5] Existentially we can speak only of "becoming" one's gender. As one of my highly accomplished friends says, she was constantly reprimanded when growing up for not "acting like a lady."

Socially correct gender performance is even more of an issue for boys. If a boy is perceived as "soft" or displays vulnerable feelings, he is told, "be a man." When a young woman fails to act like a lady or behave in a prescribed "feminine" way, still she retains her beingness as a woman. If a young boy's behavior does not conform to the male stereotype, he loses his beingness as a man. For a man to be like a woman is almost to be nothing at all.

Again, there is always danger of going too far into the blue and becoming lost there. Too much drifting and floating can make it extremely difficult to get back on course. For instance, smoking marijuana or getting high on drugs, both legal and illegal, can become a way of life. Extremely passive people who assume too little responsibility can force others who care about them to be more responsible than they desire — a seed for bitter resentment. Any form of escapism can get one "lost in the blue" and without a sense of grounding make coming down to earth painfully difficult.

I vividly remember a time when I was having trouble getting back to earth. It was two days after my first solo flight, the absolute high point for most of us learning to fly. Feeling no limitation to my power or skill and thinking I could probably "leap tall buildings in a single bound," I rented the Sundowner (trainer plane) and took off to practice my new skill.

The wind was southeast, a little unusual, but otherwise it was a nice day for flying. I had no problem taking off and none tooling around in the sky. I was feeling fantastic. The problem came in the landing. The southeast wind necessitated landing on an unfamiliar runway, and my approach was way too high and way too fast. "Pitch and power, flaps to go," was the mantra for aborting the landing and a go-around for another try. Again the approach was too high, requiring a second go-around. On the third try, I was slow enough, but the approach looked far too steep. After the third failed attempt, it was difficult to think rationally and not panic. I decided to leave the airport, fly to the practice area and try to calm down. I began to wish that I could just keep flying and not have to land the plane, but the fuel gauge was moving alarmingly close to empty. With great deliberation, I headed back to the airport and managed a landing, gaining a new appreciation that we sometimes "need to come down to earth."

Sailing into the blue, flying, being imaginative, being creative are aspects of human experience that deserve as much support as being sensible and practical. What we need to survive as whole and healthy human beings is an embracing of these experiences that often seem either-or. Jung referred to these experiences of ourselves as our Anima and our Animus — our feminine and our masculine. Since the anima is an archetype that is found in men, he reasoned an equivalent archetype must be present in women; for just as the man is compensated by a feminine element, so woman is compensated by a masculine one. [6]

Referring to our soul (anam) as masculine or feminine seems to suggest that everything about us is gender-determined. Nothing could be further from the truth, however. Some men are more identified with their anima soulfulness, some women with their animus. Gender similarities are far more pronounced than gender differences. This truth flies in the face of the popularity of notions that "men are from Mars" and "women are from Venus." Careful meta-analysis will not support these assumptions. Janet Shibley Hyde, in a study of gender similarities, says that in the realm of intimate heterosexual relationships telling people they come from different planets can imply it is impossible to communicate and resolve conflicts. With considerable data for support, she says we need to dispel these erroneous beliefs in massive, unbridgeable gender differences. Such major differences simply do not exist.[7]

So we come back to the fact that some men are more identified with the "taking in" side of themselves and some women are more identified with the "taking charge" side of themselves. The essential conceptual shift is from an *either-or* point of view to a *both-and* point of view and an acknowledgement that health and wholeness require a constant balancing of these two often disparate-seeming experiences of ourselves.

This tricky need for continual balancing can be seen within societies as well. In the land of the free and the brave, we invest much more in "masculine" defense than in "feminine" celebration of life. Without dramatic change, the attitude indicator — so much brown, so little blue — says we are headed for destruction.

Headed for destruction is where pilots go when they fly into a weather condition for which they are unprepared, lose the horizon and spin out of control. In aviation parlance, it is a matter of making the incorrect Go, No-Go Decision. Whether to go or not to go, is probably the most important choice the pilot makes, especially those of us who fly small planes. Whether we decide to take off or stay on the ground depends on many factors.

It depends on the equipment we fly. Is the plane adequate to the load we are carrying? What is the range? Is it equipped for flight in instrument conditions? Is the engine turbocharged in case the altitude of the field or the density altitude is high? Is oxygen available should there be a need to fly above threatening weather? The list goes on and on.

The decision to take off or not also depends on the ability of the pilot. Is the pilot trained and rated for flight in instrument conditions? Is the pilot current in instrument flying experience? Has the pilot performed the recent take-offs and landings necessary to carry passengers? Is the pilot current in experience for flying at night? Is the pilot free of any medication that might affect performance? Has he not had a drop of alcohol for at least eight hours? Again, the list goes on.

Most significantly, whether or not to fly depends on weather — more accurately, atmospheric conditions. And, of course, weather is highly predictable (laugh, please). The meteorologists are always accurate about the weather — yesterday's weather. It is in the forecast for the rest of today and tomorrow that uncertainty enters. Once decisions about equipment and pilot ability are out of the way, the big "go no-go" decision will depend on weather. Pilots, like sailors, become serious students of the weather to avoid unwanted surprises as much as is possible. However, because of the constant, sometimes rapid changes in atmosphere, the choice of whether one should go or not go is rarely clear. Some risk is always present in going. If one were to avoid all risk, one would never take off in the first place. Departure is always a judgment call.

Every choice in life is a choice between security (staying on the ground) and some anxiety (taking off in flight). No such thing as security exists from an existential psychological point of view. If we think we are secure, we are naïve at best and probably foolish. In seeking security, we are headed for one of the most subtle traps on life's journey.[8] Existentially, all security seeking is anxiety avoidance and an attempt to avoid death or nonbeing. Security is not part of the human condition. Have you known anyone with enough money to feel secure? Great wealth often seems to produce the opposite effect. Perhaps because there is more to lose, there is more insecurity, as evidenced by more security fences, more security guards, and more security systems!

Do we ever find the person who will make us feel secure? I have observed many people destroy a perfectly good, exciting relationship by seeking security. Far too often the focus on commitment, and all of the rules that go with that commitment, kills the spontaneity, fun, and creativity that animated the attraction in the first place. Far better to live with a bit of anxiety!

Nor does having great power to control things or other people lead to security. Perhaps because more power means more potential threat, it can bring on even more insecurity. For that reason, something like "National Security" is a promise that will never be kept.

We can of course deal with specific threats to our person, more or less. And we can deal with specific threats to our nation, more or less. In either instance it seems wise to deal expeditiously with known threats. Nevertheless, it is obvious that in dealing with known threats we have not achieved security.

On a personal level, it is sad to witness good people wasting most of their resources and the only life they have to live trying to become secure. I had a close friend who forfeited much of the enjoyment of his life by coping with every imaginable outside threat, only to be attacked from the inside. He died of cancer.

Every choice we make is a choice between some sense of anxiety or some supposed sense of security. From an existential point of view all security seeking is dying to keep from dying. It is far better to choose life and secondarily manage the risks as much as possible.

If security seeking often tempts us to stay on the ground, a self-imposed need to be at a particular place at a particular time often impels us to take off, even in adverse conditions. Clearly such an urgency impelled JFK Jr.'s flight. We are all guilty. I, too, have courted disaster with "get home itis." Most pilots have occasionally fooled themselves into a "go" decision to press on when that was unwise.

The same dynamic applies to everyday life. Often, intent on getting somewhere, we completely ignore the signs of our limited equipment, our limited abilities, or the storms we will likely need to endure. In the end, this stubborn insistence on pressing forward, mainly out of macho pride, is sadly self-defeating.

I've seen parents tear the wings off of their relationship with each other as they fly into the maelstroms associated with their children. There is a go, no-go decision to be made in each situation, and no one should be quick to judge before weighing and appreciating the complexities. However, young married people frequently encounter periods of turbulence; and usually it is best for parents not to charge into the storm. Storms pass. Even when marital difficulties appear to be chronic and long lasting, parents can risk destroying their own relationship and lives through their well-intended overinvolvement.

Patience and respect are also the most desirable qualities to have when living with adolescents. Patience here means a standard no-go policy, except when a true emergency presents itself. Respect is the essential quality of authentic relating, and lack of respect is common among parents who have difficulty believing an adolescent can make life-affirming choices or learn from choices that have been made. It takes considerable courage on the part of parents to relinquish responsibility so that their children may become responsible.

There are no hard and fast rules. Every relationship in life is unique, and every situation presents us with opportunities to choose. In flying, one learns to be flexible about choosing.

Recently, our plan was to fly from the Eastern Shore of Maryland to the Gulf Coast of Mississippi, a flight of six to seven hours. Due to other commitments, we were unable to depart until afternoon. The decision was made to get a leg on, fly to Raleigh-Durham, visit the Duke Gardens, and leave the next day for a non-stop flight to Pascagoula. (We have enough range to fly from Raleigh, but not from our home base).

Up early the next morning, we checked the weather. Bad news! The weather system to the southwest, which was supposed to pass overnight, had become stationary. All across our route of flight were thunderstorms with tops to 50,000 feet, tornadoes, hail, the works. I put in a call to the friendly Raleigh Flight Service Station to confer with their experienced weatherman. What would it be like if we were to fly due west across Tennessee to the Mississippi and then fly south toward Mobile? Long pause, then he said: "Not a very good plan." There might still be some storms popping up in that area, but even worse, there would be a widespread area of fog and mist with visibilities down to zero all along the Gulf. This was a no-brainer, an obvious no-go.

We had another concern — there was a second line of storms developing from Ohio to Virginia, blocking our route home. The best weather in the whole Eastern half of the United States was right where we were. We had a delightful day among the tulips and flowering fruit trees in the Duke Gardens. We sat quietly in the teahouse of a Japanese garden, watching a pair of Mallards tip themselves upside down and feed, a major soul-restoring experience.

Flying can help us remember that it is not nearly as important to get somewhere, as it is to celebrate life along the way. When we become overly goal-directed, we ignore our present life, the only life we have to live. We forget to savor it. To keep a balance between being responsible and being "response able" (able to respond to the pleasures of life), we need to remember to use our attitude indicator.

Chaptter Three:
Hearing Voices

I do not listen to words; I listen to feelings.

Flying in Mexico can be great fun; probably much like flying in this country was years ago. The United States today has huge areas restricted for military operations, acceptable restrictions around busy commercial terminals, and unbelievable restrictions for what seem like purely political reasons. Mexico hasn't nearly as many restrictions as the United States regarding freedom in the air.

It is a privilege to be able to fly over huge areas and spend time simply enjoying the spectacular beauty of our earth. The downside to flying in Mexico is the relative lack of radar coverage. There is no extensive Air Traffic Control standing by to hold one's hand. Pilots are more likely to be on their own than in the United States.

On this day, we had spent the first hour clearing Mexican Customs. We had learned to expect it would take about an hour and would likely involve some new procedure every time. With patience and a relaxed attitude (what else can one have in Mexico!), the experience was not unpleasant, and in the past we had established genuine friendships with several airport Commandants.

There are romantic moments in small-plane flying, two lovers alone in an intimate cockpit at 11,000 feet, a landscape barren of human habitation below, the deep azure blue of the Gulf of Mexico on the left, the rugged seemingly haphazardly arranged Sierra Madre Oriental mountains on the right. We were filed to Jalapa, with an alternate route along the coast to Veracruz. Then, halfway to our first reporting point, Tampico, the romantic mood dramatically changed. Carolyn remarked with apprehension, "Oil is streaking up the windshield." Observing oil leaking from the engine is something that immediately gets a pilot's attention! My first words were unprintable. Then I thought, "The engine is going to quit any minute, so let me see where we might land." A careful study of the charts showed nothing. No houses, no roads, and of course no airports. There were many flat places to land, but then what? My training told me: "Use all available resources." Perhaps the man at the Tampico airport, to whom I was to report, might know of some uncharted airstrip. I called, explained my emergency, and asked, "Do you know of any airfield between my position (one hundred nautical miles north) and Tampico?" A concise answer came back: "Cleared to land any runway." That was not exactly what I wanted to know, so I asked again. I got the same answer: "Cleared to land any runway." I said to Carolyn: "Ask him in Spanish." She did and got the same answer in Spanish, "Cleared to land any runway."

Suffice it to say, there were some tense moments before the runway at Tampico loomed into view. When we had landed, an army truck loaded with ten young soldiers, automatic rifles at the ready, met us. The Mexican government is a bit suspicious of someone landing at an airport other than the one on the flight plan. The soldiers filed out, circled the plane, looked at the windshield and grinned, got back in their truck and drove away.

The resolution of this part of the tale is anticlimactic: The friendly airport Commandant secured a mechanic who quickly diagnosed our problem: a blown gasket on the oil dipstick. With typical Mexican ingenuity, the mechanic made a new one and we were again on our way to Jalapa — a beautiful mountain city, with a university, a first-class symphony orchestra, and a spectacular anthropology museum.

Here is where the story enters the realm of *Never Again*. Never again will I do what I did next.

Because we had been delayed, we arrived at our approach to Jalapa later than anticipated, and the weather had changed considerably. A stratocumulus cloud layer was forming beneath us, widely scattered at first, but becoming more solid. Reports were giving the ceiling as 6000 to 7000 feet, and we could observe the tops as being around 9000. We were filed IFR (Instrument Flight Rules) at 11,000 feet, so there was not likely to be any problem in landing at Veracruz, a coastal town with good instrument approaches.

However, we wanted to land at Jalapa, a small friendly airport with no instrument approaches and avoid a terrible two-hour cab ride on narrow, winding, mountainous roads with a macho driver. The plan was to obtain an IFR clearance to descend through the clouds and, once under the deck, cancel IFR and fly VFR into Jalapa, believing we would still have a good 1000 to 1500 feet of ceiling over Jalapa (elevation 4800 feet). That was the first time I heard a warning voice that I ignored. In hindsight I know that I felt fear as surely as a deer senses a stalking hunter more than a mile away. Nevertheless, I told myself that my plan was perfectly reasonable.

Under the clouds and still some thirty nautical miles from Jalapa, we began to enter more rugged terrain. We identified a river and a canyon, which we determined, having been there before, would lead us to Jalapa. Again, I was hearing warning voices, louder this time. In the recess of my mind, there may have been an echo from Antoine De Saint-Exupery, "Blind flying through a sea of clouds in a mountain zone is subject to the severest penalties… A pilot in trouble who buries himself in the white cotton-wool of the clouds might all unseeing run straight into a peak."[1] But I convinced myself that this look-see approach was perfectly reasonable.

Now, picture what it might be like flying up a canyon with mountains on both sides and overhead clouds becoming lower and lower. And the space available within which we can fly was fast diminishing.

At this point a voice began screaming, "*climb out of here!*" But I kept looking at the DME (distance measuring equipment) that showed only six miles to the airport, so I pressed on. I had read many accounts of pilots flying into a blind canyon, running out of options and plowing into the side of a mountain. I always thought: How dumb! I would never do anything like that.

But I did.

I had now boxed myself in, and there was nothing left to do but climb as fast as possible up into the clouds. It was back to the three basics: Aviate, Navigate, Communicate. That meant throttle full, climb at best rate of climb; make a quick guess at which way to turn; ask Veracruz for an IFR clearance to on-top conditions.

The challenge was in the navigating part. I was not that sure of the path out through the mountains. I knew Orisaba was to the right. As a matter of fact, before we had descended below the clouds, we had both remarked at the beautiful sight of this magnificent 18,000-foot mountain standing snow covered above the clouds.

We turned to the left, climbing at fifteen hundred feet per minute, when suddenly the clouds parted: We were heading straight into the side of a mountain! We were so close to collision I actually thought I could smell the coffee beans below — a terrifying moment that still comes up in a dream, one of those dreams you don't want to remember, but keep remembering anyway. I made a quick evasive turn. Miraculously, we missed the trees and rocks. Saint-Exupery could not have been wiser: "The machine which at first blush seems a means of isolating man from the great problems of nature, actually plunges him more deeply into them."[2] How we avoided being a deadly CFIT (controlled flight into terrain) statistic is still hard to believe.

We continued with a clearance to on-top conditions, reactivated our original IFR flight plan, and landed at our Veracruz alternate. What is absolutely clear, however, is that without that miraculous parting of the clouds, this tale would not be told.

What can we make of all this? ***Listen to the voices***. That may not be as schizophrenic as it sounds.

Indeed, sometimes schizophrenia may not be as insane as it sounds. As Thomas Sasz once observed, we need the sanity of the insane to show how insane our sanity is. [3] I know something of the truth in that statement because I spent two-and-a-half years doing an internship and residency in a large federal mental hospital, working closely with men who were *called* schizophrenics, an insensitive way to refer to deeply troubled human beings. These men taught me a great deal about myself, and about listening

I had a Norwegian supervisor whom I viewed as rather weird. In retrospect, I realize he was smart and uncommonly creative. The first assignment he gave me was to interview Mr. H, who had been diagnosed as Schizophrenia, Catatonic Type. According to the records, he had not spoken or related to anyone for more than fifteen years.

Interviewing Mr. H meant taking two attendants on the ward with me, leading Mr. H to an interview room and placing him in a chair. It was an excruciating experience for me to sit there, with no acknowledgement of my presence, and talk. I do not know what I talked about — probably the weather, what I knew to be going on in the world, and other general nonsense. Fifteen minutes seemed like hours, and it was as much as I could stand.

I had no idea what this assignment was about but dutifully reported to my supervisor that I had completed the task. He replied, "fine, and you will need to be doing that every day for a while." My exact reply was probably, "the hell you say!" He said, "It is either this or you are out of the program." I think at that time I probably said, "OK, then I'm out."

Having slept on it, however, I came back determined to endure what I believed was cruel and unusual punishment because this was the best clinical psychological internship in the country. I did the best I could with my time spent with Mr. H and gradually became more comfortable with the silences. This had been going on every day for about three weeks, when during the "interview" Mr. H moved his eyes ever so slightly to look at me. It's strange to relate how something so slight could have felt so exciting. As I sat with my legs crossed the next day, he reached over and squeezed my shoe and said: "I once had some dancing shoes."

From that day Mr. H began talking with me, explaining that he did not care much for what people said. Instead, he said, "I listen for feelings." Later he revealed that he had chosen to talk to me because he sensed that I cared what he felt. I asked him to join my weekly therapy group, and he agreed. Many times I would get lost trying to follow what was happening in the group; but when I would ask Mr. H, he knew exactly what was going on.

In the psychiatric records Mr. H was listed as unpredictable and perhaps dangerous. There had been occasions when he had suddenly hugged or kissed people who came on the ward. Occasionally, he had slapped people. Mr. H explained that he kept very still and quiet so that he could tell what others around him were feeling. When he encountered people filled with unusually strong love or hatred, he could not help but react. Lacking any better explanation for his behavior, the psychiatric records reported that Mr. H "heard voices."

On another occasion he said, "You know, Dr. Snyder, these psychiatrists here are crazy." In some cases I had my suspicions, but I was more than a little curious about why Mr. H would say so. When I asked, he said simply, "They believe what people say with words." Another time he said, "I don't listen to words, I listen to feelings."

By this time I was beginning to understand the true meaning of my assignment. I had focused too much on words, on that left hemispheric "masculine" side of myself, and I needed to become receptive to the right hemispheric, intuitive "feminine" side. My habitual focus was on what patients were saying, and in my attempts to analyze and explain, I had failed to appreciate the feelings being expressed. Once I tried to enlist Mr. H to teach me how to be still and to pick up the feelings of others. I was sitting beside him on the ward, as still as I knew how, when I heard him quietly saying, "You're moving too much."

Much of the time we are in too much of a hurry — moving too much — to attend to that other, feeling side of ourselves. I certainly failed my lesson on that flight to Jalapa. Intent on strictly following the logical side of myself, and deaf to the intuitive voice of warning, I came perilously close to doing us in.

Functional schizophrenia can be viewed as the result of living constantly in a relational environment of mixed messages. The words being heard and the behavior being seen are the opposite of the feelings being experienced.

In my group of so-called schizophrenic men, the subject of mothers came up. Mr. X said, "I once asked my mother if she loved me." Mr. Y asked, "What did she say?" Mr. X replied, "She said, (Mr. X speaking with a loud, firm voice) of course I love you." This being a group of supposedly crazy people, Mr. Y repeated his question, "What did she say?" Mr. X responded, "You are absolutely right, I never wanted you. You were an unwanted child, and you ruined my life."

In some attempt to maintain my own sanity, I decided to be around on Sunday afternoon to observe Mr. X's mother, described in the medical records as a loving woman who visited her son regularly, often bringing fresh-baked goodies. The clues that something was wrong were indeed subtle. She spoke pleasantries but appeared terribly uncomfortable around Mr. X. She made no serious effort to connect with him physically or emotionally and clearly wanted to leave as soon as she reasonably could.

Accepting ambivalent feelings toward one's own child is extremely difficult. To compensate for not wanting the child, a parent can become over solicitous and overindulgent. However, the parent's words and behavior can often ring hollow. An approach toward the child that, on the surface, appears loving can be felt by the child as entirely false.

This pattern is not confined to parent-child relationships, of course. Any emotion that we consider unacceptable can give rise to a counter-phobic reaction, leading us to behave diametrically opposite to the way we are really feeling. On the receiving end of this dynamic, the point is: Hearing voices can be a way of experiencing feelings that are not being owned by the person with whom we are relating. Because the trusted side of ourselves is often the rational, controlling self, we dismiss these feelings we are sensing as having no basis in reality. Yet there is this inner dis-ease telling us that we are missing something important. In all close relationships, feelings are communicated whether or not we intend to share them. When the words and behavior are opposite to the feelings communicated, we are propelled into a schizophrenigenic dilemma. This experience of the dichotomy between words and feelings, when chronic, is the primary cause of functional schizophrenia — it tends to make one feel crazy.

A marriage can become a dangerous place to be when this type of communication habitually occurs. A common and serious example of such a crazy-making experience happens when one partner is having an affair and vociferously denies that anything is going on. What is the suspicious spouse to do? Trust the words of denial or trust the feelings of dis-ease? As with a person who is called schizophrenic, expecting someone to believe the reality of one's feeling experience is likely to elicit a "you're crazy" response. If we hear words and see behavior that is opposite to the feelings we are experiencing, we become extremely disoriented.

In many smaller but sometimes equally serious ways, we can cause those close to us to feel crazy. We do this by laughing away a friend's insecurity with us when we know precisely why that insecurity exists. We do this when we argue that our motives are pure and know that our intent is exploitive. We do this when we know exactly why our partner might be feeling scared and deny that we have done anything or are about to do what could fully explain the fear.

One of the first rules for intimate relating is *do not make your partner crazy*. This inevitably requires making ourselves anxious and being as real and authentic as we can be. It takes courage to choose to be as open as possible about where we are, who we are, and what is really going on within us. At a minimum it means acknowledging anything we know that possibly could be eliciting what our partner is feeling. In psychological jargon it means, "giving a reality base to the feelings" to free the person from a schizophrenigenic bind ("being made crazy").

In the end, a capacity for intimacy always depends on having sensitivity to feelings, ours and those of others, and much of psychotherapy is designed to help us achieve just such sensitivity. However, having sensitivity makes us more vulnerable to experiencing conflict between the felt messages and the verbal ones. We can end up like Mr. H, listening to feelings, not listening to words. That is, we become more sensitive to being made to feel crazy. [4]

Chapter Four:
Unusual Attitudes

Do not project out of your experience. Project out of your desires.

The airplane is absolutely out of control. We are spinning round and round, heading straight for mother earth. The ground that covers the windshield seems to be coming up too quickly to possibly be avoided. The voice in my headphones (coming from the sadistic instructor behind me) says, "OK, John, it's your airplane." Now, if I had time to think and shout, I would surely be screaming: "Hell no, you idiot! You got us into this horrible mess, you get us out!"

Instead, I employ the mantra that has been hammered into my head during the last few days: *Push, Power, Rudder, Roll.* By this time, I am supposed to have the "muscle memory" to (1) push on the yoke to unload the stalled wing, (2) reduce the throttle since we are going down, (3) step on the sky, that is, push with full authority on the rudder pedal that is on the sky side of the airplane, and (4) smoothly roll the wings to level.

Of course, all of this has to be done very quickly, in a much shorter time than it takes to write this. It works like magic: I employ my mantra

(Push, Power, Rudder, Roll) and the airplane stops spinning, the nose comes up, we level off and are back to flying normally. This ability to recover from such an unusual attitude had taken hours of practice and some moments of screaming terror.

The most nonintuitive aspect of this mantra is the first move: push on the yoke. It does not take long in flight training to get the hang of this "yoke" (which resembles a car steering wheel). If you push forward, the plane starts heading nose down; if you pull back, the nose of the plane heads up. After a while, this reaction becomes instinctive, sometimes in odd circumstances. During a time when I was flying every day, another car suddenly stopped in front of me while I was driving in heavy traffic. I instinctively pulled back on the steering wheel as hard as I could; apparently thinking I could go up and over the car in front of me. It did not work.

The optional flying program that I had been taking, Unusual Attitude Training, focuses intensively on understanding stalls. Airplane stalls have little to do with engine failures, something many news reporters seem to have a hard time understanding. The airplane stalls when the wing has too little air passing over and under it to provide lift. If the wing stops flying (stalls), the plane stops flying and can very soon be spinning toward the ground.

So here we are spinning toward the ground. I need to push forward on the yoke. Everything in my head cries NO, but by now I have this "muscle memory," as they call it, and some confidence in the concept. It does work. As they say, "First, get the wing flying."

The Unusual Attitude Recovery program also trains us to be proficient in getting ourselves out of situations before they become disastrous. One thing that can and sometimes does happen is that the plane becomes literally upset, sometimes flipped inverted, by wake turbulence. Wake turbulence is a horizontal vortex of wind (like a horizontal tornado) that develops behind the wing of a large, heavy airplane. In the special training, we learn how to right ourselves with a minimum loss of altitude. Much of the training lies in judicious use of the rudder. In the Trinidad, the modern plane I fly, one can become somewhat lazy in attention to the rudder. Normally, nothing serious will go wrong. Part of the training in recovering from runaway trim (the autopilot going haywire) requires that I take my hand off the yoke, hold both arms over my head, and keep the plane in a slow circle around the horizon by use of the rudder alone — an amazing experience.

All of this is to say that many things can go wrong with airplanes; and, as Murphy's Law reminds us, if things can go wrong, they likely will go wrong...and at the worst possible time. It does not help to stick our heads in the sand and simply hope for the best.

But we certainly do that with relationships. I would like to suggest that becoming intimately close to someone is much more dangerous than flying. We have a way of ignoring just how much unhappiness, how much outright pain and suffering take place in our intimate life relationships. Most obvious are cases of physical abuse, but I am talking about something less acute, more chronic. I mean all those hours, weeks, and years of awful estrangement from others that men and women and children live with and endure.

The best way to understand estrangement is to see it as the opposite of intimacy. Estrangement is feeling distant, cut off, disconnected, alone, abandoned. Such estrangement becomes the seedbed for hostile interaction, attacking and defending, sulking and withdrawing, and just plain meanness. The result is little happiness or satisfaction in being with the person to whom one is nominally close.

Intimacy, on the other hand, is feeling close, safe, trusted, loved, desired, respected — the very things that we all most deeply desire and long for. When we are feeling truly close to someone, there never seems to be enough time; and we are willing to make great sacrifices to experience such moments of closeness. Those are the times when the cares of the world seem to vanish, and we allow the beauty of life to overwhelm us.

You get the picture. We would like to be flying along blissfully, but suddenly we fly into turbulence that threatens to flip us upside down. We can stall the wing that gives us the lift and quickly enter a graveyard spin. In thirty-five years of helping people in upset recovery, I have been privileged to learn a few things that can be distilled into a mantra similar to "Push, Power, Rudder, Roll."

Like aeronautic upset recovery, recovery from unusual emotional attitudes also requires four things: (1) Knowing what one is feeling, (2) Expressing that feeling to (3) Someone who understands that feeling, and who (4) Identifies with the feeling. Like the "Push, Power, Rudder, Roll" routine, this is much more easily said than done. Gaining proficiency takes lots and lots of practice. Stay with me, as I take more the voice of a teacher and we look at each of these four steps in turn.

Knowing What You Feel

The capacity to relate intimately to another person absolutely depends on Step #1: knowing what we are feeling. At first glance, this may seem very simple. However, to assume we know what we are feeling without giving the matter our attention is like naively assuming the wing will keep giving lift no matter what our attitude. American culture today places little importance on attending to one's feelings. We are perpetually busy doing things. Feelings merely seem to get in the way and make it more difficult for us to accomplish our larger goals.

It used to be that when a couple experienced a loss of intimacy and an increase of estrangement, the woman would be the first to seek help. Jung believed that women were more likely to be in touch with the intuitive, creative, emotionally oriented side of themselves. For our purposes here, we will call this the Anima, Right Hemispheric, "Feminine" side of ourselves. To the degree that gender and hemispheric dominance coincide, women are more likely than men to first be aware of their feelings, be disturbed by a lack of intimacy and want help in overcoming any estrangement in their personal relationships or marriages.

The first task, therefore, would be to involve the husband, male partner or in a same-sex relationship, the more left-brained person. Men, Jung believed, were more likely to be in touch with the other side of themselves, the side that is managing, competitive, organized, and likes to get things done. For our purposes, we will call this the Animus, Left Hemispheric, "Masculine" side of ourselves.[1] When achievement is the goal, there is tremendous advantage in being able to put feelings aside, even though doing so diminishes one's capacity for intimacy.

Before you excitedly disagree, let me say that referring to these two sides of ourselves as masculine and feminine has nothing to do with gender. I am using the word "masculine" and "feminine" rather differently than Jung did. Like a growing number of people in the United States and Western Europe, I take a more social constructionist view of gender, a view that does not see Animus/Anima as coextensive with biological sex. I continue to use the terms "masculine side" and "feminine side" as a kind of imagistic shorthand, however. These words carry feeling — indeed, useful discomfort. They create a picture of the distinct psychic states we need to keep us in balance, just as a plane needs a differential airflow on both sides of its wings to keep it flying. As I said before, thinking of Animus/Anima in this way can help us move from an either-or view of men and women to a both/and view that more accurately describes the emotional complexity of actual human lives.

Today, it is sometimes the man, not the woman, who first seeks help because a relationship has lost its former intimacy. Perhaps he desires more closeness with his wife or is aware of estrangement growing between her and their children. In such instances, the therapist's first task is to involve the wife, who may be a successful, highly achieving woman, a bank president or partner in a law firm, or the like. In such relationships, the woman may be more identified with the Animus component and the man the Anima; it is the woman who may have lost touch with her feeling "feminine" side and the man who may need to become more assertively "masculine."

We need to recognize the wholeness of our experience, as I observed before. We need to be able to move into the managing (masculine) side of ourselves to get things done; and we need to move into the feeling (feminine) side of ourselves to enjoy life and become intimate with others. Ideally, this movement from managing to feeling should be fluid, spontaneous, and even unpredictable.

Lack of flexibility in moving from the managing (Animus) approach to life to the feeling (Anima) approach creates a serious block to intimacy. For either the man or the woman a capacity for intimacy depends entirely on being sensitive to feelings.

This brings us back to Step #1 in attitude recovery: paying attention to feelings. If we do not know what we are feeling, we will not be able to consciously express those feelings, and we will be blocked from experiencing intimacy.

We have already seen how feelings get communicated in close relationships, whether we want them to be or not. And we have seen that if these feelings are not owned, we can make our partner a bit crazy. How can you train yourself to be more aware of feelings? There is no easy answer. It often involves a profound attitudinal change. The first step might simply be to ask yourself many times, day and night, *what am I feeling?* Carry a 3X5 pad and write down the answer at least once an hour throughout the day. Sometimes it helps to visualize a color to represent the feeling. Color associations can bypass left-hemispheric thinking and capture varieties of nuance. On one occasion, with an artist client, this suggestion caused some difficulty. I didn't know how to spell half the words he used. What a wonderful color vocabulary! It is amazing to discover how little feeling vocabulary most of us have developed. A word of caution: If the association is more than one word, it is probably a judgment, not a feeling. "I feel hurt" is sufficient to express the feeling and hopefully will elicit empathetic exploration. "I can't believe you could be so insensitive as to humiliate me that way in front of the children," is a judgment that will likely become the opening salvo in an attacking and defending battle.

Finally, all feelings are transitory. There is a flowing quality to feelings. They come and they go. Present progressive is the most appropriate tense for the expression of feelings. This is not a lesson in grammar. This is a fact about communication. The most powerful way to express feelings is to say what one is feeling at any given moment. And this approach supports exciting freedom of expression. "I am not liking you at all right now." Picture this response: "I don't blame you, you would have to be crazy for liking me just now, I have been such an ass." Or this could be the expression: "I am feeling an incredible desire for you," pause, "don't worry about it, it will go away!" Another example: "I've been feeling so much love for you (all day) or (since we got away from the kids) or (right now) or (because you have been so understanding) or (because of the way you are looking at me).

I'm talking about real communication. "I love you" doesn't cut it. "I love you" often falls flat because it comes across as plain vanilla generic feeling. We must seize the moment when feelings occur and express

51

them with directness and authenticity. Because feelings are transitory, we can easily miss the opportunity.

The bottom line: Our capacity for intimacy with others depends on spending time, energy, and attention on ourselves, increasing our awareness of exactly what we are feeling, and taking on the anxiety that comes with its expression.

Expressing What You Feel

Expressing feelings doesn't seem particularly difficult, but it can mean breaking lifelong habits of carefully protecting ourselves. Aside from the exposing our vulnerability and the anxiety that provokes, the very act of expressing feelings can seem to come out of nowhere. Modern life is so cluttered with external stimuli, few moments remain for the quiet contemplation we need in order to focus fully on what we feel. For most couples, creating a context for an exchange of feelings means getting out of the house. Taking a quiet evening walk can help, as can finding a romantic corner in a restaurant or coffee shop or spending a night at a remote B & B (without clocks, TVs, radios, etc.). Simply being gone from Saturday noon to Sunday noon can provide quality time for sharing feelings. There are many other creative ways to make the shift from our habitual left hemispheric managing way of life to our sensual side. Little things can have a big effect on the quality of our lives: stopping to smell the crisp fall air, savoring the taste of a strawberry, listening to a warbler sing, feeling the bark on different kinds of trees, watching the changing colors of a sunset.

We often read about the importance of expressing so-called "negative" feelings — feelings of resentment, irritation, and unhappiness. But without some transition to the right hemispheric world, we lack context for the expression of what we might call "positive" feelings — feelings of desire, satisfaction, pleasure, and love. These feelings often have no context and alluding to them can be quite awkward. We need to create an atmosphere of freedom to support the expression of sexuality and playfulness. It helps to consciously devote energy to creating a mood for those spontaneous expressions of delight partners can find with each other. Intimacy requires this sense of warmth, and even familiarity.

We need also to make ourselves anxious and express what we call "negative" feelings. Negative feelings are any emotions we would rather not feel, or dislike feeling, or are afraid of feeling. As I'll explain later, whatever we are feeling always has a basis in our experience. There is no possible way we could be feeling anything other than what we *are* feeling. And, despite our fears, an honest exchange of these emotional realities is genuinely satisfying for both partners in a relationship.

The point here: To experience the intimacy and closeness we desire, we have to pay attention to our feelings and find ways of expressing them. *There is no other way to experience intimacy.* There is no neutral place. Without intimacy, relationships move rapidly out of control into a graveyard spin toward estrangement.

So again, having a close relationship means: (1) Knowing what we are feeling, and (2) Expressing that feeling.

Expressing Feelings to Someone Who Understands

Knowing and expressing what we feel is the giving side of a relationship. There is a receiving side in relationships as well.

When feelings are being expressed, it is imperative that they be received in an understanding way. Unfortunately, "understanding" can sometimes seem weak or even condescending — like a pat on the head, that implies, "I understand, dear." The root meaning of the word suggests otherwise, however: "to stand under." True understanding is a powerful act of support. Picture yourself literally standing *under* and supporting your partner — around, under, and behind — helping your partner to express all that s/he is feeling.

Such openness to understanding is an inviting stance. "I understand that you are feeling resentful about the money I've been spending on golf. Could you say more about that?" When the feelings about a particular incident seem exhausted, you can then enlarge the invitation: "Is there possibly more that you are feeling resentful about? Please talk to me." The understanding person is there to make it safe for the other person to express feelings. The invitation needs to be completely free of judgment. We need to assume that there is good reason for the person to be feeling whatever s/he is feeling. Either there is a basis for the feelings that we can discover with a little patience, or the person is crazy. As tempting as it might seem at times to go for the second explanation, I suggest that we always rule it out.

"I can understand that you feel unfairly treated by my spending so much on golf lately, and I suspect there may be other ways in which you have been feeling unfairly treated. I care what you feel, and would like for you not to be feeling so resentful. What do you suggest we do?"

That may sound very saintly, and it might be hard at first to picture such a non-defensive response to a direct expression of resentment. It's a little like pushing forward on the yoke of the airplane when one is heading straight for the ground and certain death. But we are talking about survival skills here. Anything we do is better than getting in the vicious cycle of attacking and defending that leads to estrangement.

As I observed before, the first rule of intimate relating is: *Do not make your partner crazy.* That means we need to have patience and take the time to discover the reasons for whatever our partner is feeling. Once we have that understanding, the other important issue is: Do we care what he or she is feeling? If we can show understanding and caring, we can establish closeness. Without that understanding and caring, we are lost. An intimate relationship is impossible.

Identifying With the Feeling Expressed

It is not enough that we understand the feeling being expressed by our partner. We must also be able to *identify* with the feeling. We must be able to project ourselves into our partner's sensibility. Identifying with another's feelings is no small feat. We have not had the exact same experiences our partner has had, but as human beings we have the gift of projection. With some help from our partner and an openness on our part, we can imagine what it must be like to be experiencing whatever he or she is experiencing.

One thing is certain: Nothing is more estranging than to take risk in expressing feelings to someone who says, "I understand what you are feeling, but I cannot imagine feeling that way myself."

This need for identification is especially important across sexual lines, since men have not grown up female, any more than women have grown up male. Empathy requires a sustained invitation to become acquainted with another person's interior life, as well as some understanding and familiarity with the developmental issues of the opposite sex.

Sullivan had a nice saying: "We are all more basically human, than otherwise."[2] That is, being human is more significant than being old or young, being black or white, being male or female. He was once overheard saying to a patient: "There is no feeling you are having now, ever have had, or ever will have, that I have not also experienced."

In an era of "identity politics," Sullivan's stance might seem offensively reductive. There is nothing more infuriating than being told "I understand, dear" by someone who is utterly clueless about what we've just been through — someone who is carelessly conflating another human's life with his own. Nevertheless, Sullivan's approach can be extremely powerful *if* we make the crucial distinction between *experience-as-behavior* (what we have done, what has been done to us) and *experience-as-emotion*.

Each of us is biologically and experientially unique. Distinctions of class, ethnicity, nationality, sex, and sexual orientation profoundly shape how we see the world. Even people who grow up in very similar environments can experience their environment very differently — just as pain tolerance differs dramatically from person to person. My dentist says he often is confused about this: "I can be doing exactly the same thing and one person is fine, and the next is in agony."

Existentially, however, none of us is unique. We are all in the same death-bound boat — by turns vulnerable, fearful, and full of joy. And we all use a similar palate of feelings to respond to the things that happen to us. In our interactions, if we keep focused on expressing what we have *felt*, rather than what we have done or thought, then true understanding is possible, even across great gulfs of cultural difference.

The fourth step in attitude recovery — identifying with the feeling expressed — is thus dependent on that crucial first step: knowing what we feel. The ability to be response-able, to stand under other people, begins with our ability to understand ourselves. We need to grow empathy in our own hearts before we can export it to our relationships. If we pause in our busy lives and take the time to get to know our feelings, the payoff is enormous. Knowing what we feel allows us to scare ourselves by expressing our feelings to others and experiencing their support and identification. Only in this way can we have the intimacy and closeness that each of us so deeply desires.

One of the obstacles to an open expression of feelings in relationships is that we often confuse feelings with thoughts or judgments. Again, this is not semantic quibbling; it reflects the need to differentiate two quite opposite ways of relating. One way leads to distance and estrangement; the other leads to closeness and intimacy. The difference is crucial.

For example, imagine that Carolyn says to me, "You never pay attention to me any more." Then imagine that I respond defensively: "How can you say that? We were together all afternoon the other day. When was it? Thursday? Friday? I'm doing the best I can. What with that crisis with your brother, handling a practice, this writing project, what more can you expect?" (Tone of voice: If you were thinking not just of yourself, you would not be dumping more on me tonight.)

This is not an uncommon way for two people to interact; it is not pleasant and can escalate into something fierce in no time.

What actually happened? Carolyn said, "I'm feeling a little lonely and neglected." That expression of feeling made it easy for me to move toward her and say, "I can understand that. Most of my energy has been going to other places, and I was so engrossed in this writing project I have to admit I was not even aware you were here. I'm here now."

This dialogue makes me look very good. Trust me, we do not always get it right. As a matter of fact, I have painful memories of relating to my partner defensively as in the first scenario. Over the years, however, we've become more and more aware that judgments (such as you're not paying attention to me) are likely to illicit a defensive reaction and that expressing feelings (such as I'm feeling lonely) will illicit a feeling response. Such vulnerability presupposes that one is relating to someone who cares what one feels. With sufficient data to the contrary, one had better be prepared to defend oneself in the best way possible! If we desire closeness and become convinced the other person does not care what we feel, the only sensible choice is to end the relationship.

Unfortunately, even when people obviously do care deeply about each other's feelings, they can sometimes lose the picture that the other cares. Relating becomes reduced to fighting or painful silence and distance. Unquestioned projections determine the experience and an overriding judgment stands in the way of exploring new avenues of feeling. "If you cared what I feel, you would be doing A, B, C." Or the corollary: "You cannot possible care what I feel or you would not be doing X, Y, or Z." If put in that defensive position, how many would have the courage to come forward with a feeling response?

Much of our daily focus is on behavior: Are we doing what we judge we *should* be doing? Are others doing what they *should* be doing? There is nothing wrong with performance contracts. More or less explicitly we make them all the time. We put in a good day's work; we expect to be paid. It would be a little silly for the employer to say that he did not feel like paying us. If we pay the shop, we expect to have our car repaired. We have lawyers to ensure contractual performance. But to bring these behavioral expectations into an intimate relationship is as ridiculous as a person at the flight gate saying, "I don't feel like honoring your ticket."

Unless we relate to others with the expectation that our feelings matter, it is highly unlikely we will experience our feelings being received and responded to. A basic and important principal for living: *Do not project out of your experience. Project out of your desires.* If we picture out of past negative experiences, we are likely to keep reinforcing that same experience. We can easily believe we know the truth of how things are. Projecting out of what we have been experiencing binds us to no change, no movement, no growth. If, on the other hand, we identify what we desire and picture out of those desires, we open ourselves to some exciting possibilities. "It is a startling truth," writes O'Donohue, "that how you see and what you see determines how and who you will be."

Psychotherapy with couples works well much of the time simply by providing a context within which two people can begin to see each other differently and begin to picture having what each desires. The most significant shift is an act of trust, a belief that the desires and longing being expressed truly matter to the other person. Whether the couples are male-female, male-male, or female-female, choosing to trust is the same. Relational dynamics know nothing of sexual orientation.

Trust is an active choice, and choosing to trust someone tends to make that person trustworthy. I had an experience the other day that provided a simple lesson in the reciprocity of trust, though one not fraught with great consequence. I frequently obtain ice for our sailboat from an ice machine on the highway. On this occasion a note on the door read, "Machine broken, open door, help yourself." Inside were blocks of ice and a box full of quarters. Being so trusted was making quite a few people very trustworthy that day.

In emotional relationships, it is even more important to choose to trust: "I choose to trust that you care what I feel, and I will find some explanation for your behavior. I will continue to assume that whatever you are doing or not doing does not reflect insensitivity to my feelings." Of course, we are making ourselves vulnerable in assuming this stance, just as the man with the ice machine was making himself vulnerable. Intimate relating entails vulnerability. Protecting ourselves from potential hurt and disappointment will not work because it takes us into the darkness of distant estrangement.

The capacity for intimacy is totally dependent on the extent to which one is willing to make oneself vulnerable and drop all defensiveness.

It is possible that this understanding might not by itself offer much practical help. Pilots are required to read about spin recovery and take many tests; but I never had much confidence that merely *knowing* what to do to get out of a graveyard spin would be enough in an actual emergency. That is why I signed up for the Unusual Attitude Recovery training, to practice the right moves until they became instinctive.

Spin recovery in intimate relationships requires similar training. To gain proficiency in coping with the unusual attitudes and upsets that are inevitable in human life, you might need to hire an instructor. And practice, practice, practice. And then, practice some more.

Chapter Five:
Uncontrolled Fields

If we feel enough to get angry, we feel enough to cry.

Easton field still relied on the old NDB instrument approach in the 1990s, not the best way to get down through the clouds, try to find a runway, and put the plane back on terra firma. This way of searching for the ground was designed more than sixty years ago and relies on, of all things, an AM radio signal. But at the time, it was all we had.

After three and a half hours in the air, we were arriving from Chicago's Palwaukee airport following a visit with my sister. Easton airport was reported to have a ceiling of nine hundred to one thousand feet and a visibility of two to three miles. I pictured what I wanted to do: fly with reference to instruments through clouds until fairly close to the ground, then hopefully break out in the clear under the clouds with enough forward visibility to find the runway and land. The low cloud ceiling and limited visibility in fog and mist meant that the airport was marginally VFR (open for flying under Visual Flight Rules).

We had broken out of the clouds at slightly under a thousand feet and were on a five-mile final to the runway when all hell broke loose. Two pilots, one of whom had called out his position ahead of us, "base to final twenty-two," and one who was flying without a radio, came within inches of colliding, avoiding that catastrophe only by seeing each other at the last possible minute.

By the time we had completed a "missed approach" and come back around for our second approach and landing, we saw two airplanes pulled off helter-skelter onto the grass and two big men who appeared to be on the verge of mortal combat.

This was an unusual sight. The pilot fraternity is, almost without exception, one of the most courteous and friendly groups of men and women in the world.

A typical example of that courtesy occurred when our plane lost electric power near Detroit. An unnamed pilot, delaying his own flight, had circled above us the whole time we were in trouble, in case he might be needed to relay our messages to ATC.

Why, then, were two pilots on the ground giving way to uncontrolled anger and aggression? Before I analyze this business of uncontrolled feelings, it might help to say a word about Uncontrolled Airports to our nonpilot readers.

People who fly exclusively in commercial planes might reasonably suppose that all airplanes are under the guidance of Air Traffic Control. Much to the chagrin of those of us who have been flying for some time, the control and limitation of our air space has dramatically increased. In fact, however, only about ten percent of the more than five thousand public-use airports in the country are actually commercial airports with control towers. The rest are Uncontrolled Fields, though as such they are not inherently unsafe. Pilots fly by standard patterns, give standard position reports to each other, and the rule to "see and avoid" other planes works quite well usually.

The usual was absolutely not working on this day.

Whether anyone should have been flying around Easton with such low ceilings and visibility without being on an ATC controlled instrument flight plan was unclear. Flying without a two-way radio was even more questionable, as these radios are now easily affordable. Nevertheless in this particular case, it is possible that everyone was behaving legally, if not sensibly. Unfortunately, as in many areas of life, what is legal and what is sensible are not the same.

Embracing anxiety and being foolhardy are not the same either. Richard Collins, an aviation writer whom I trust as much as anyone who writes about flying, likes to point out the obvious risk in any kind of flying. He thinks it foolish to attempt to convince people that flying is without risk. The best approach, according to Collins, is to *manage* the risks, which seems a pretty good way to approach life.

A blissful unawareness of risk led these two men to get themselves in a near mid-air collision and scare the hell out of themselves. They almost killed each other in the air and seem to have been hell-bent on trying to kill each other once they got on the ground. Easton had become an uncontrolled field in more ways than one. There was no air traffic control, and there was no personal anger control. Why would such explosive anger erupt between two ordinarily well-behaved and gentle pilots?

Obviously we get angry when we feel scared or hurt or helpless or some combination of these basic feelings. Hurt, fear and helplessness are "primitive" feelings that we all have felt at some time or other, though no words prove adequate to express all that we feel. When we *get* angry we are reacting to feelings of vulnerability in an attempt to eliminate their cause. A common reactive stance to frustration or helplessness is first to become angry and then super controlling. When I was younger, I once felt so frustrated during a homeowner's project that I punched a hole in the wall. "Good job, John!" A common reactive stance to fear is to get angry and attempt to eliminate what we believe to be the source of our fear, as the two pilots were trying to do. A common reactive stance to hurt is to get angry and become, in turn, extremely hurtful.

Hurt, fear and helplessness are impossible to avoid. There is no way to be alive in the world without experiencing these feelings, sometimes in ways that overwhelm us. However, although reacting with anger to feelings of helplessness and frustration is characteristically human, it is also true that as human beings we can make *choices* about an appropriate response.

Many psychologists say that to be healthy we should express our anger — "ventilate" — get it out. Not everyone believes this, however. Carol Tavris, in a well-researched book, <u>Anger: the Misunderstood Emotion</u>, critiques the view that expressing anger is liberating: "It seems to me that the major side-effect of the ventilationist approach has been to raise the general noise level of our lives, not to lessen our problems. I notice that the people who are most prone to give vent to their rages get angrier, not less angry. I observe a lot of hurt feelings among the recipients of rage. And I can plot the stages in a typical 'ventilating' marital argument: precipitating event, angry outburst, shouted recriminations, screaming and crying, the furious peak (sometimes accompanied by physical assault), exhaustion, sullen apology, or just sullenness. The cycle is replayed the next day or next week. What in this scenario is 'cathartic'? Screaming? Throwing a pot? Does either action cause the anger to vanish or the angry spouse to feel better? Not that I can see." [1]

Those of us involved in relational therapy see this pattern of defensive anger repeated all too often. When psychotherapy was viewed as a process between an individual and a therapist, this destructive pattern of expressed anger was often obscured. Indeed, there was a time when it was considered a breach of ethics for the therapist to have contact with anyone in the patient's circle of relationships. For the classical Freudian analyst, such contacts were virtually taboo, although Freud himself egregiously violated his own principal on occasion.

Beginning with the teachings of Harry Stack Sullivan in the early fifties [2], therapists began to broaden the therapeutic context and include significant others in sessions with the patient. Sullivan in *The Interpersonal Theory of Psychiatry* taught that any deformation of our personalities arose in significant relationships and that any reformation could best be achieved by involving the significant others, if possible. The principal role of the psychotherapist was to create a meaningful and healthy relationship with the troubled individual — a model on which other reconfigured relationships could be based. Sullivan, and what came to be known as the Washington School of Psychiatry, opened the door to new therapeutic interventions designed to address the psychological intricacies of the unhealthy relational dynamics that had shaped the patient's personality.

In the early 1960s Sullivan's insights began to have an impact on the way therapists viewed anger. My work at the time was focused on deeply depressed people who had been institutionalized for treatment. The prevailing Freudian view was that depression was the result of suppressed rage and for the person to become whole, this rage had to be released. Freud's worldview was based on a hydraulic model of fluids. If blocked in one area, the flow of energy would push out in another. The goal was to remove the blocks. This model is essentially true when applied to suppressed or repressed feelings; however advising people to ventilate their anger is generally contraindicated because anger itself is a *denial* of feelings. Indeed, it is a form of repression — and thus a *source* of depression.

In the short term, ventilating anger often seemed to work with some depressed patients. If the depression resulted from "sitting on" anger and rage, I and my colleagues at the time encouraged depressed patients to release their anger; after they did, some became well enough to leave the hospital. Although these people left still very angry, we were usually unaware of the problems this anger subsequently created. We tended to pay little attention to the calls from the distressed spouses, or other family members, who had become recipients of this released anger.

Eventually, however, a few of us began to suspect that both anger and depression might be reactive states of denial to the primary feelings of hurt, fear or helplessness, and we began to experiment with a two-stage process. We would support the depressed person in getting angry, and then explore the feelings of hurt or helplessness *behind* the rage. This was a more time consuming process, but it worked. At the time "ventilating" one's anger was too ingrained a theory for us to see the obvious. By helping the depressed person get in touch with the suppressed hurt, fear, or helplessness, we could have bypassed the angry stage all together.

Once we were able to shed what we had been taught, the truth became clear: *Anger is not a feeling.* Feelings are transitory. They come and they go, and the healthy stance is simply to feel whatever we are feeling. Anger is something we call on to keep ourselves from feeling. Anger is a defensive reaction designed to protect us from exposure to vulnerability. Our language is instructive, in this regard. The usual expression is "I *got* angry," not "I *felt* angry." On close examination, when we say that we *feel* angry we are likely describing a different experience. Substituting other words, such as I felt "hurt" or "frustrated" make more sense.

The dynamics of anger are clear and predictable. Defending ourselves against feelings of vulnerability, we get angry. The recipient of our anger feels hurt and vulnerable and usually defends by becoming angry in return. Then we increase our defense and become even more threatening. When does the escalation stop? It is no surprise that anger and violence have an underlying connection.

Understanding the hidden source of anger has implications for every level of human engagement including international aggression. Tragically, when attacking and defending escalate beyond a certain point, nonviolent solutions become difficult to envisage. The horror obscured by the impersonal word "escalation" becomes clear only when we see directly what violent aggression does to individual bodies and lives — as I did recently when I met with distraught parents whose son had been seriously wounded in Iraq.

Interestingly, when we feel strongly enough about something to get angry, we also feel strongly enough to cry. As children, before we were talked out of it, whenever we felt hurt, we cried. Whenever we felt scared, we cried. Whenever we felt helpless and alone, we cried. And there is nothing wrong with this same direct approach for us adults. Expressing what we feel at the exact moment we feel it is the path most likely to elicit the response we long for: to be cared for and comforted.

Lest this advice sound naïve, I should add that crying and expressing hurt usually is not the best advice to give a battered spouse. Nor is crying the right thing to do when the soldier is afraid and being shot at. Nor is it a quick fix for the Middle East conflict. If the goal is to eliminate the enemy, then getting angry is the way to go.

Anger can be used positively to galvanize our legitimate defensive response when under physical attack. Some form of anger is also legitimate when we are outraged by injustice, cruelty, bigotry or senseless violence. When we feel appalled, disgusted or incensed, we are still presumably consciously in control of ourselves. The ability to choose to express feelings is, existentially, one of the most precious attributes of human beingness. Choosing to get angry might seem a contradiction in terms. Anger is commonly viewed as "loosing one's temper," which is more descriptive of what happens in our reactive stance. The very nature of reaction is absence of conscious choosing. A profound difference exists between reacting with anger and healthy confrontations.

Harmful and potentially destructive reactive anger is different from a healthy assertiveness of oneself designed to establish boundaries or to set appropriate behavioral limits. Such assertiveness is conscious, deliberate and respectful both of oneself and the other, and can be expressed strongly: "I feel most unfairly treated that I have to wait for you so often when we have agreed on a time to meet! I deserve more consideration than this!"

Establishing boundaries to designate appropriate behavior is crucial for parent-child relating and is no less important for adults. Any boundaries we wish to establish need to be reasonable and fair and open to question. Often there are far too many rules that one is never to question. As we shall see later, existentially the only rule is whether one human being is exploiting another, treating the other with a lack of respect, or in any way dishonoring the other's human beingness.

Confronting unfair treatment, establishing behavioral boundaries, expecting to be respected while respecting the other — all are entirely appropriate. However, this relational dynamic is quite different from reactive, out-of-control anger which, consciously or unconsciously, intends to hurt and or annihilate the other.

My primary concern is with the relational dynamic of this reactive anger. Anger expressed toward those near and dear inevitably leads to emotional estrangement. From an existential perspective, intimacy is about having friends, and estrangement is about having enemies. Living with an enemy is inherently problematic and dangerous. It is even more frightening to realize that the enemy is oneself.

Angry estrangement in relationship with others often signals a more basic estrangement from the tender side of ourselves. That is why Abraham Maslow [3] could observe that the creation of man's enemies begins with his human twin, woman. An either-or orientation to our personality structure — either anima or animus, soft or hard, assertive or compassionate — inevitably creates estrangement within ourselves. One of the crucial goals of therapy, as Maslow recognized, is to move from this dichotomizing and splitting toward an integration of seemingly irreconcilable opposites.

Cultural norms that dictate a separation and alienation from vulnerable feelings (Anima) result in a male-gender dominant society in which women are second-class citizens, if citizens at all. Alfred Adler stated emphatically that this ranking of one half of humanity over the other half poisons all human relations. The underlying problem is not men as a sex; rather, it lies in an accepted system in which both men and women are taught to equate true masculinity with violence and dominance and to see men who do not conform to this model as "too soft" or "effeminate." [4] This alienation and estrangement of one half of oneself from the other, and one half of humanity from the other, leads to a distorted view of human nature as inherently angry, aggressive, violent.

To counter this view of human nature, the American Psychological Association has endorsed the "Seville Statement," composed by an international group of prominent scientists from many disciplines who met in Seville, Spain in 1986. They reached a consensus that it is scientifically incorrect to say that humans have inherited a tendency to violent or aggressive behavior. In all well-studied species, it has been found that status within the group is achieved more by the ability to cooperate than by aggressive behavior; and although we do have the neural apparatus to act violently, nothing in our neurophysiology compels us to do so. [5]

In a convincing way, Riane Eisler [6] traces the development of the still prevalent hypothesis that human beings are predetermined toward anger, violence, and aggression. She found that our "true" nature is more inclined toward cooperation with others and respect for everyone and everything around us, a propensity distorted by historians accustomed to defining history exclusively in terms of conflict, wars and conquests. In early cultures, divine power was originally depicted in female human form. In such societies, "effeminate" qualities such as caring, compassion, and nonviolence were highly valued.

Eisler believes that the shift from a partnership to a dominator model of social organization has been a gradual but predictable process. As increasing numbers of "invaders" encroached on agrarian societies, brute power, strength, and weaponry became paramount instruments of conquest. "At the core of the invaders' system was placing a higher value on the power that takes life rather than the power that gives life. Despite this trend, there are powerful exceptions to the over-glorification of the "masculine." For example, Eisler comments, Jesus taught his followers to elevate the "feminine" virtues from a secondary to a primary role. Instead of toughness, aggressiveness and dominance, he urged mutual compassion, gentleness, and love. [7]

"Our everyday life is much stranger than we imagine, and rests on fragile foundations," writes Paul Seabright, an economist. Why is everyday life so strange? Seabright sees evolution at odds with what would have seemed, as recently as 10,000 years ago, to be our evolutionary destiny. It was only then that "one of the most aggressive and elusive bandit species in the entire animal kingdom decided to settle down. In no more than the blink of an eye, in evolutionary time, these suspicious and untrusting creatures developed co-operative networks of staggering scope and complexity — networks that rely on trust of strangers. When you come to think about it, it was an extraordinarily improbable outcome." This cooperation and trust of strangers is, he says, what has made modern economic life possible. [8]

What can we make of all of this? Returning to my opening flying story, we can conclude that: In many places in the world no air traffic control exists. In many places in the world, anger control is lax or nonexistent. As when flying to an uncontrolled field, cooperation and trust are essential. The goal in intimate relating is trust and, if not anger elimination, certainly anger management.

When we are in a close relationship with another person, the best way not to get angry is to embrace the feelings *behind* the anger and express the hurt or the helplessness or the fear. Few of us, myself included, are able to eliminate every initial angry reaction, however much insight we might have. What we can do, after getting angry and uttering a biting comment, is ask ourselves what we are actually feeling. For me, ninety percent of the time I feel helpless or frustrated; the other ten percent I feel hurt. If we can identify and express the hurt or frustration, the initial attack ceases to become estranging.

Much is at stake in being able to eliminate anger from our lives. Not only can we avoid those long hours and days of living in dark estrangement from those important to us; we can also live longer. Study after study shows convincing links between anger and essential (chronic) hypertension and coronary heart disease. Suppressed anger also contributes to stress, tension, high blood pressure and heart problems. While this might seem to imply that outwardly expressing anger is the solution, remember that becoming angry has the same harmful result as does repressing one's feelings.

An increasingly common non-medical consequence of uncontrolled anger can be seen in the phenomena of "road rage." The AAA Foundation found that between 1990 and 1996, 12,610 injuries and 218 deaths resulted from an unmanageable anger behind the wheel of a car. Working with couples, I have observed another result: The helpless suffering of a passenger when a driver goes momentarily berserk. One such outbreak can ruin an evening with friends, the whole day, or an entire vacation!

Getting angry destroys relationships, ruins our health, drives us to become increasingly reactive and marginalized. Again there are rare occasions in our lives when getting angry may be the right thing to do, but getting angry in a relationship with someone who cares about our feelings is never the right thing to do.

He came in furious, shaking with rage: "I'll tell you how the weekend went — terrible! We were in her college bookstore and she couldn't find enough stupid things to buy, a sweatshirt for her father, mugs for her sister, stuffed animals for her nieces; I thought she would never leave. She felt my impatience, and do you know what she had the gall to say, 'I would think you would appreciate how much fun I am having.'"

Some months earlier they had visited the bookstore of Bob's college. Margaret had become annoyed that he was taking so much time and had been critical of his purchases, saying they did not have money to waste on such nonsense. Outside the store, in front of the children, Bob had reacted with such anger that a passerby had called the police.

It was this incident that precipitated the call for couples' therapy.

"I didn't say anything to her because we have this deal and I'm not to get angry. I agree, that getting angry makes me the bad guy and I hate it. But when I held back I felt sick like I might throw up." "Sounds like you were swallowing something you could not digest," I said, "can you recall what you were feeling at the time?" Pause. "I just felt so damned unfairly treated." Pause, shoulders hunched forward. "This happens so often, it hurts." Because he looked as if he might cry, I said, "Makes you want to cry, huh?" Big shaking sobs broke loose. At some point, almost inaudibly, he asked, "Who cares?" Handing him a box of tissues, I said I thought that was a pretty good question and asked how he was now feeling. Red-eyed he said, "actually kinda good, thanks." "Would you like to have Margaret come up and join us and perhaps explore whether she cares about your hurt?" "I'd like that," he said.

This change in their relationship was facilitated by Bob's efforts not to indulge his reactive anger and by Margaret's growing awareness that her judgmental approach did not invite expression of feeling. It was not easy for Bob to move into that softer, vulnerable feeling side of himself. However, Bob's choice to drop his angry defense made sense once he could anticipate a caring nonjudgmental response. In turn, Margaret's willingness to move to a more inviting stance became possible once Bob's angry reactions ceased — reactions of which she had been deathly afraid. A negative feedback loop had been transformed into a positive feedback loop.

Diane brought her "uncontrollable" teenage daughter Bonnie to see me because, more and more, "she lies." After spending some time getting past Bonnie's sullen, angry demeanor, I began to experience an engaging young woman with a good head on her shoulders and a delightful sense of humor. At a session with the two together, Diane began immediately with the latest instance of Bonnie's lying. It seemed that Bonnie, after promising otherwise, had met with George, with whom her mother thought she had become too serious (read "sexual"). Diane was adamant that George was not the sort of person with whom Bonnie should be involved. Because Bonnie had been open with me, I knew that she privately agreed with her mother and was in the process of ending the relationship.

Acting with respect for both Diane and Bonnie, I posed a choice. On the one hand, we could see this situation through a moral lens and judge Bonnie as a liar and bad. On the other hand, we could view this interaction differently and observe that Bonnie was not being open because she did not perceive her mother as someone with whom it was safe to be open. Diane interjected several times, "you don't understand, she lies," then suddenly she seemed to understand. She softened and began expressing her fears and worries; Bonnie relaxed her defense and began tentatively to share more openly.

Relating well to another person means choosing to relate with openness and respect. Relating with trust and openness is natural and pleasurable for us as human beings. We become closed only when we experience or anticipate negative criticism or judgments. Unfortunately, much of our relating is behavior-based, contractual, and thus inappropriate for the expression of feelings. However, we also enter emotion-based relationships where it is worth the risk to suppose the other person cares about us, even if we have doubts.

For the third time I was taking my car to be repaired for the same unresolved problem. I was already furious and about to lose my fragile control when the man at the counter told me they could not take the car because two mechanics were out sick. Just then Jim, the service manager, walked in, a man with whom I had been relating for years. Without prior thought, I found myself expressing how hurt and disappointed I felt that I could not get my car repaired. I probably expressed more than I had intended. I surely felt like crying. Jim responded by putting his hand on my shoulder and saying, "we'll take care of it. Do you need a ride back to your office? We'll bring the car when it's ready." Feeling a little embarrassed but grateful, I accepted, blubbering something about being willing to reschedule the service if he was in a bind. Despite my own desires, I cared how Jim felt. It's easy to imagine how differently this scene would have gone had I gotten angry.

Again, getting angry creates estrangement and can ruin both our relationships and our health. On rare occasions, getting angry might be the right thing to do; but getting angry at someone whom we can reasonably suppose cares about our feelings is never the right thing to do.

The right thing to do when we can reasonably expect understanding is to allow ourselves to be vulnerable, express the feelings of hurt, frustration and rejection, express how unfairly treated we feel, and how afraid we are. Opening ourselves is not only the right and healthy way to relate, it is also the deeply satisfying way to relate.

Chapter Six:
Head Winds/ Tail Winds

If I did not leak a little every day, I would drown in my tears. [1]

One hundred and sixty-five knots on the air speed indicator — normal enough at our power setting and altitude, but the ground speed is deteriorating dramatically: 130 knots, 115 knots, 95 knots. It doesn't help at all when Carolyn points out that a truck below on the Interstate is gaining on us.

We are over the West Virginia Mountains, flying as low as we dare because the head winds are even stronger the higher we go. The view is spectacular. Rhythmic ridges in diagonal lines capped with white snow on western slopes contrast with dry gray to the east, providing a breathtaking, surreal, view of nature. We have ample time to take in this wonderful winter scene as we plug slowly along on our way to Texas. Texas! If you know the geography and know we are flying from the Eastern Shore of Maryland, why, you might wonder, are we flying northwest over West Virginia, when Texas is south-southwest? The detour is necessitated by a winter storm over the direct route, with predicted icing in the clouds. We know from previous brief encounters that we do not want the plane to resemble anything close to an icicle. A wing does not continue to fly that way, and we depend on her; so keeping her happy is a number one priority.

So here we are, traveling slowly at 90 knots in the wrong direction, in a machine that is supposed to save us lots of time going from point A to point B. Head winds!

Of course there are also tail winds. You think these two would balance each other out. However, any pilot, or any sailor for that matter, can tell you that the odds of that happening are no more in your favor than the odds in casino gambling. Considering the law of averages, bet on the head winds. Tail winds are a long shot.

Sometimes you win. On one occasion, flying home from Sea Island, Georgia, we picked up a great tail wind. It was fantastic to see 230 knots register on our ground speed. We were over Charleston, South Carolina, in no time; then Myrtle Beach, and before we had settled in our seats, we were approaching Richmond, Virginia. Between Richmond and home, we heard the Richmond controller talking to a Delta flight inbound for Washington: "Delta 1234, I need to slow you down a lot for spacing. Slow to 150 knots. You will have a *Trinidad* passing you on the right." Wow! That's a bit like a Chihuahua outdistancing a Greyhound.

The true irony of this discourse is that there are *no* head winds. There are no tail winds either. At least in the way we usually think of wind as air rushing past us from the front or back. The airplane is not experiencing any wind blowing at her nose or tail. She is simply in a medium that is moving. The air aloft is moving, and she is helplessly being carried forward or back, wherever the air chooses to take her. Flying a plane allows us to navigate about in this moving medium, but we soon learn to respect the power of the medium and to acknowledge our limitations in moving within it. A presence of an ambient medium need not disappear once we touch ground.

So intent are we in our daily lives on getting from point A to point B that we often ignore the fact that we are actually in a moving medium. This channel vision is the result of a strong left hemispheric "masculine" emphasis on getting somewhere, getting something done, exploiting all the resources available to attain a goal.

We tend to give far too little attention to the Anima side of our experience — our connection to the moving medium within which we inescapably find ourselves. The poet John O'Donohue notes that: "There is labyrinth within the soul.…. Below the surface of our conscious awareness a vast rootage determines our actions…This unconscious is a powerful and continuous presence." [2]

Speaking of the unconscious, Jung said, "we are always surprised afresh to discover that something can jump upon our back or fall upon our head out of mere nothingness, radically altering the pattern of our individual lives."[3]

People differ on what the "unconscious" means or whether it even exists. However, in a recent article entitled "Freud is Back," Mark Solms [4] reports that respected neuroscientists now say their findings confirm not only the existence, but also the pivotal role, of unconscious mental processing. (Psychologists and neuroscientists have often held antagonistic opinions.) For some researchers in the field of psychology one sensible approach has been to hypothesize an unconscious aspect of personality — to assume there's more to who we are than we can ever consciously know — and then to test this hypothesis experientially. In a similar vein, I propose we image our lives as taking place in a moving medium, as an airplane moves through the air or a boat moves through the water.

Our cultural reliance on psychotropic drugs can be read as one of many attempts to deny the existence of a moving medium, a living space through which we move, an energy field of essential reality. One researcher examining the efficacy of the most popular SSRI (Prozac) found that the true drug effect is so small that it is questionable whether it should be called an antidepressant: "the success of SSRI's represents a triumph of marketing over science."[5] Nowhere is this more evident than in our over-concern with "mood disorders." The way this condition is medically defined suggests that nearly everyone is "bipolar." We seem to have lost any appreciation for the normalcy of mood swings — our personal moving medium. Life has its headwinds and tailwinds. Sometimes life is an uphill struggle. Sometimes we are coasting downhill with the wind at our backs. Do we really desire to flatten our moods to a dull, safe sameness?

The pharmacological solution is especially problematic when we examine the connection between creativity and so-called madness. Many of history's creative geniuses would today be diagnosed as bipolar. Many were, in fact, diagnosed as manic-depressive, the old term. The downside of the mood could sometimes be medically altered, but at the cost of any up side and a loss of creative drive. Understandably, some of these creative men and women stopped taking their medicine. Having had the privilege of knowing some extremely creative people, I have witnessed how daunting a medical approach can be. Many creative people report that when they use psychotropic medication, they experience a loss of the emotional intensity necessary to spur their creativity. The drugs interfere with clarity of thought and diminish the artists' energy and enthusiasm for work. A treatment plan designed to minimize the use of mood altering drugs is essential for such people — indeed, for people in general, extensive psychotherapy often is quite effective and without the harmful side effects.

In *Touched With Fire* Kay Jamison, psychiatry professor at Johns Hopkins, explores the link between creativity and madness: "Many highly creative and accomplished writers, composers, and artists function essentially within the rational world, without losing access to their psychic 'underground.' Others...are likewise privy to their unconscious streams of thought, but they must contend with unusually tumultuous and unpredictable emotions as well. The integration of these deeper, truly irrational sources with more logical processes can be a tortuous task, but, if successful, the resulting work bears a unique stamp, a 'touch of fire,' for what it has been through."[6] Of Lord Byron, for example, Jamison writes: "aspects of his underlying temperament often worsened into periods of painful melancholia and disruptive, perturbed mental states... His temperament also, however, made him exquisitely responsive to virtually everything in his physical and psychological world; it gave to him much of his great capacity for passion and understanding, as well as for suffering." [7]

Listening to Robert Schumann's Cello Concerto in A Minor, one of the masterpieces of the cello repertoire, it is difficult to conceive that such dramatically moving and passionate music could have been composed so close to Schumann's attempted suicide and hospitalization for a depression from which he never recovered. In a far opposite mood, Schumann wrote, after publishing his first composition: "I doubt if being a bridegroom will be in the same class with these first joys of being a composer. The entire heavens of my heart are hung full of hopes and presentiments. As proudly as the doge of Venice once married the sea, I now, for the first time, marry the world." On another occasion, Schumann said: "I am so fresh in soul and spirit that life gushes and bubbles around me in a thousand springs." [8]

The poet William Blake also describes the interplay of highs and lows eloquently:

> Joy & Woe are woven fine
> A clothing for the Soul divine;
> Under every grief & pine
> Runs a joy with silken twine. [9]

Even when a person's dramatic mood swings are clearly pathological and even if it could be established that the problems are genetically determined, it is far from clear what should be done. Certainly, we should be careful not to use pharmacology to eliminate the future Van Goghs, Virginia Woolfs, and Schumanns — to use these names to represent all those struggling souls in art and literature and music.

Perhaps some of these artists could have been helped by modern medicine without debilitating side affects, and in some cases the drugs are absolutely necessary to prevent suicide. Having spent time on the "back wards" of mental hospitals in the sixties, I am not so naïve as to deny that mood disorders can include serious pathology. Severely depressed people deserve all the help they can get. The problem is our cultural tendency to expect pharmacology to supply an easy answer. In the words of a physician-poet, "if the disease had a cure, we would not need so many remedies." [10]

Speaking for the scientists in pharmacology, Mark Solms believes "the time will come when people with emotional difficulties will not have to choose between the talk therapy of psychologists, which may be out of touch with modern evidence-based medicine, and the *drugs prescribed by psychopharmacology, which may lack regard for the relation between the brain chemistries it manipulates and the complex real-life trajectories that culminate in emotional distress.*"[11] Having been for years involved with "the complex real-life trajectories that culminate in emotional distress," I appreciate the acknowledgement that complex real-life trajectories exist and need to be addressed. Studies have shown that a combination of drugs and psychotherapy is sometimes the most effective course of treatment. However, prominent advertisements for mood altering drugs obscure the relational factors that generate emotional distress and present solutions in an exclusively mechanistic fashion. Thomas Sasz believes that mental illness is often used to obscure and explain away *problems in personal and social relationships*, just as witchcraft was used for the same purpose from the early Middle Ages until well past the Renaissance. [12]

Help for emotional distress can also come in wholly unexpected ways. A curious remedy occurred around the time of the American Revolution at Eastern State Hospital in Williamsburg, Virginia, where I worked a couple hundred years later. During the winter a group of depressed patients was being taken across the grounds from one building to another. Their attendants led them on a short-cut across a frozen pond. The ice proved to be too thin, and the whole group fell in. Immediately they all recovered from their depression! That was the beginning of "shock therapy."

A member of my own family experienced another, even more extreme treatment for depression. An aunt, whom I knew well, became seriously depressed when my cousin, her only child, was killed in the Battle of the Bulge in Germany. Nothing seemed to relieve her immobilizing depression, and she was eventually given a prefrontal lobotomy. Her treatment was considered successful, as those treatments go. The recovery period was long, but she functioned adequately to a nice old age. However, after the lobotomy, a definite flatness permeated her moods. Observing the same flatness of mood in many people taking the latest designer antidepressant drugs, I wonder whether we have merely developed a more sophisticated form of lobotomy, albeit a less permanent alteration of personality.

We need to distinguish between truly crippling mental disorders and the mood swings of normal life. The distinction is becoming blurred because of our deep cultural uneasiness with, and general objection to, strong feelings. We object to such feelings for at least two salient reasons: Because feelings get in the way of our accomplishment mentality, and because feelings can make us anxious. Feelings take us where they will; we are not in control; we are in a moving medium.

If we were to let ourselves feel as sad as we sometimes need to feel, how would we accomplish whatever we need to accomplish? What would prevent us from becoming hopelessly lazy and indolent? What would prevent us from drowning in our feelings?

So much of the difficulty we create for ourselves comes from our objecting to what we are feeling. As I observed earlier, all feelings are transitory. Feelings come and feelings go. It is the feelings we do not wish to feel — the feelings that we object to feeling — that we keep inside ourselves. These are the feelings that cause us trouble, those that we "sit on," that we repress and suppress. As John O'Donohue observes: "Our lives would be immeasurably enriched if we could but bring the same hospitality to meet the negative as we bring to the joyful and pleasurable. In avoiding the negative, we only encourage it to recur."[13] He also alludes to a strange paradox of our experience: if we try to avoid or remove the feelings we object to, they will pursue us. We have seen earlier how suppressed feelings can actually motivate our behavior. It takes great energy to push these objectionable feelings back and keep them there. This is energy we need for living. Without this energy we become depressed.

When it results from unrelenting suppression of feeling, depression is not transitory. It does not come and go. The depression is there as long as we refuse to feel whatever we are fighting. In that regard, it might have been better to say that my aunt was suppressing too much sadness than to say that she was depressed. My aunt was profoundly stoical, and my uncle even more so. In their household there was little, if any, place to weep or moan. My aunt was fully entitled to feel much sadness and resentment. In one especially poignant moment she exclaimed to my sister, "I know what they are trying to do, they are trying to make me forget Dick. I don't want to forget Dick." Her son Dick had been an Eagle Scout, an "A" student, a fine athlete, a good boy. He had graduated from high school in June and been killed in Germany only seven months later. Our physician-poet observed, "There's nothing medicine can do to solve the riddle of love's suffering."[14] In such painful circumstances as in the loss of a child, to bottle up feelings is a recipe for emotional disaster.

I know a woman, a poet, who experienced a tragedy similar to my aunt's. Her teenage son died suddenly after an ordinary bike ride. He died some years ago, but she has not gotten over it. Why should she? She says she often still cries in the shower. Is she not entitled to her sadness and loss? A bright, energetic person, she experiences great bursts of energy when writing her poems. Like most artists, she disclaims responsibility for her inspiration, "it is as if I am moved to express myself, I experience no choice about it." At those moments there is no question but that she lives in a moving medium.

With her permission, I quote:

> Life's lies lie
> Waiting to be known —
> Hidden under rocks of Christ
> and moralistic stone.
> Discovered by surprise,
> when a child dies,
> Held up in the face of my
> "Gone where?" "Gone why?"
> Soothing lullabies — coping tools
> "His time to go," "God's will abides."
> Who is fool enough
> to uncover life's lies? [15]

John O'Donohue tells of a friend who experienced himself in this moving medium: "He had flu during the winter and the loneliness he had repressed came out to haunt him. He got desperately lonely; instead of avoiding it; he decided to allow the loneliness to have its way. He sat down in the armchair and gave himself permission to feel as lonely as he wanted. As soon as he gave that invitation to his soul, the loneliness just poured through him. He felt like the most abandoned orphan in the cosmos. He cried and cried. In a way, he was crying for all the loneliness in his life that he had kept hidden. Though this was painful, it was a wonderful experience for him. When he let the loneliness flow, let the dam burst within, something shifted in his relation to his own loneliness."[16] This is an excellent example of how to not fight life's head winds!

Transferring one's understanding of moving mediums from air passage to water is easy. My own transition went the other way, from sailing to flying. Whether in the water or in the air, the movement of the medium has to be considered and respected. I remember one time attempting to make passage through an open drawbridge when the current against me was seven knots and my available top speed was six knots. The result was predictable! On another occasion we were sailing from Grand Manan Island to Nova Scotia in the Bay of Fundy, where tides run thirty feet or more. With that much water moving back and forth, there is no escaping the fact that we are in one hell of a moving medium.

In *Moments of Being* [17] Virginia Woolf used the water analogy to describe her experience in a moving medium: "I am a porous vessel afloat on sensation, a sensitive plate exposed to invisible rays...taking breath of these voices in my sails and tacking this way and that through life as I yield to them." Similarly, Herman Melville reflecting on mankind said: "We mortals are all on board a fast-sailing, never sinking, world-frigate, of which God was the shipwright; and she is but one craft in a Milky-Way fleet, of which God is the High Admiral." [18]

We create a considerable tension for ourselves when we fight the flow of our feelings, refusing to believe that we are in a moving medium, and fail to respect the powerful forces within which we live that push and pull us about.

Gerry and Anne were in acute distress when they scheduled their session. Their bedroom had become a place of excruciating pain because of the feelings they experienced in any romantic or physically intimate interaction. This was especially true for Anne, who had experienced sexual abuse in her childhood and adolescence. She had not been penetrated or physically injured, but a lot of men had poked their penises at her — a stepfather, an uncle, an adult male friend of the family — all experiences that were disturbing, conflicting and impossible to understand.

Gerry, in contrast, had grown up in a sheltered home and subculture, in which people lived by strict behavioral codes. He described himself as something of a nerd in high school, someone who rarely dated and did not see himself as attractive to the opposite sex. Gerry had a strong need to be desired.

Herein lay the dilemma: any expression of passion on Gerry's part was met with explosive anger from Anne. For Anne, the surge of feelings coming up [19] was similar to the feelings she had experienced when she was abused — another penis being thrust toward her. Gerry would get angry and shout, "you're making me feel like a dirty old man" and withdraw to another room.

Anne and Gerry were living in a moving medium that was creating great distress. Old suppressed feelings were determining their current feeling experiences. Anne eventually came to understand that some extremely powerful feelings could come up for her around any experience linked to her earlier sexual abuse. Once her expression of those feelings to Gerry was tearful rather than angry, Gerry was able to encourage and support her. "Touched," as he said, by her pain, he became tender and loving. Later he shared with Anne how undesired he felt and how familiar and painful feeling undesirable had been for him, especially in his formative adolescent years. In experiencing Gerry's pain, together they were both able to cry. When Gerry and Anne understood that their powerful, long withheld feelings were not problems to be dealt with but opportunities for a special understanding and closeness, the moving medium ceased to be a swirling current in which they feared they might drown.

We move through life in a medium of powerful feelings that need to be embraced. "Embrace" might seem an awkward word to use for emotional experiences that have been the source of trouble, embarrassment and disdain. Nevertheless, we can be certain that, given adequate consideration, we will discover that whatever the feeling, it is a feeling we are especially *entitled* to feel.

As I observed in the opening flying lesson, respecting the moving medium requires an open, flexible attitude. Preset expectations about how best to accomplish a task, when we will arrive at where we desire to be, even in what direction to head, all require constant readjustment. We give too little attention to the need for this kind of flexibility and, as a result, create enormous tension for ourselves.

Tension results from an inner conflict among our judging, feeling, and behavioral functions. We create tension every time we will ourselves to behave contrary to what we feel because we *judge* this behavior to be what we need to do, what we *should* do. Such inner tension produces stress that harms us. Researchers familiar with the human immune system say that, next to getting sound sleep, reducing stress is the most important consideration in maintaining a healthy body. Living with too much tension and stress lowers immune functions and makes us susceptible to all sorts of physiological problems and illnesses.

Ignoring that we are living in a moving medium, ignoring the feeling we are walking around with all of the time and allowing stress to accumulate, is nothing like the experience of anxiety that we examined earlier. Yet we find the words "tension" and "anxiety" commonly used as if they were synonymous. This is not mere quibbling over words. What is at issue is a need to differentiate between two very different human experiences — anxiety, which is necessary for healthy living, and excessive stress or tension, which can be deadly.

Some of this confusion between stress and anxiety comes from the fact that the same drugs might be effective in reducing either one. However, physiologically it is possible to distinguish between what happens within us when we feel anxious and what happens when we experience prolonged stress. With anxiety comes a definite adrenaline rush. Perhaps we retain some collective unconscious memory of being a little creature about to be eaten. In any case, *anxiety* can result in a mobilization of energy to run like hell or fight like hell, as if our survival were at stake. Examples of the adrenaline rush that comes from risk-taking are endless. Indeed, some people say it is addictive. On the other hand, when conflict arises among our thinking, feeling and behavioral functions, *tension* is experienced as physical tightness. Most of us can probably locate where our bodies tighten with tension. By learning to distinguish these two states, we become better able to take on the anxiety that enlivens us and better able to drastically reduce the sort of stress-producing tension that can lead us to an early death.

A practical exercise to help yourself recognize stress is to periodically stop and free associate: "If I were to do what I feel like doing, I would... tell off my boss!"

How free you are in allowing expression of whatever wants to come up determines the value of the exercise. For example an honest, spontaneous response to being in a long, hot, boring meeting might be:

"If I did what I felt like doing, I would scream and run out of here!" You probably wouldn't want to act on these impulses, but at least you would know that the tension was building inside you, and know why. The rule is: The stronger our feelings, and the more we are willing behavior that is not in accord with our feelings, the more tension we will be experiencing.

Am I saying we should just do whatever we feel like doing? Of course not. I try to live a civilized life — although, I have to admit I sometimes envy my Siamese cat. She seems to get along very well, living her life doing whatever she feels like doing.

Many times in life we must act in ways that are contrary to our feelings, for very good reasons.

Being aware when we are making these choices and knowing the price we pay in tension is an insight that can help extend our lives. We are likely always to be feeling more than we know, and to move strongly against what we are actually feeling can be dangerous. It is far more sensible to adjust our heading, paying attention to the headwinds and tailwinds, accepting the moving medium in which we reside, and being aware of the powerful feelings moving us this way and that.

Unfortunately, there is very little cultural support for going with the emotional flow — often described pejoratively as "moodiness." Unpredictable shifts in mood, from high to low and back again, are a normal part of living in an unpredictable universe; but this existential truth of our human beingness tends to make us anxious, so we deny it. Moreover, mood swings can sometimes seem extreme and frightening.

Returning from the big annual air show at Oshkosh, Wisconsin, I was dodging cumulous buildups near Chicago. Flying at 13,000 feet, I could see the tops of these towering white clouds to be around 20,000 feet, but they were scattered, and I was expecting to fly between two of these thunderstorms directly ahead. Then without warning, Chicago ATC assigned me a new heading that was much closer to one of the storms. Despite my pleas, ATC could not issue a deviation because there was heavy air traffic in the area. Being much closer, I could now see I was on a collision course with one of the dreaded monster storms, so it was clearly tighten-seat-belt time. Being inside the cloud was a nightmare: 3000 feet per minute up, 3000 feet per minute down, and hail — loud banging hail — with blinding flashes of lightning. It all felt like I was riding a bucking bronco determined to throw me to my death. My training was to attend to only one thing — keep the wings level — otherwise the stresses would literally break the plane apart. I was tempted to turn back out of the storm, but I knew that was a definite no-no. "Keep straight ahead and you will come out on the other side," they had told me. And sure enough, that happened. After probably no more than five or ten minutes, my wrestling with chaos was over and I broke out into some of the most beautiful clear sky I have ever seen.

As Saint-Exupery once said, we don't know how to talk about the violence of a thunderstorm except by piling one adjective on another. We therefore recognize our powerlessness to convey what we have been through and give up on the idea of describing hell.[20] Going through such an experience Carolyn says is not unlike a couple in a close relationship experiencing a fight.

Mood swings can certainly be like that. Trying to fight the updrafts and downdrafts of life can cause an emotional crash. In these times of emotional extremes keeping the wings level and riding out the storm is scary, but it works.

In our culture, however, it often seems safer to reach for a pharmacological quick fix, a modified lobotomy; disable the parts of the brain responsible, put life on an even keel, flatten out the fluctuations of mood, dissolve the highs and lows. In recent years, both doctors and patients have been increasingly sold on the idea that "mood swings" are inherently pathological and completely avoidable, with proper chemical tinkering. Putting life on an even keel has become synonymous with proper adjustment, despite evidence of significant side affects including a diminution of libido or life energy and any sexual interest.

Unfortunately, it has become customary to assume that some disturbance in the brain causes the symptoms of depression. Unfortunate, because from a logical perspective, it is quite possibly the other way around. What if depressing ourselves causes measurable changes in brain chemistry? It would follow that in learning how not to depress ourselves we could avoid the pharmacological choice and circumvent the flattening side effects of drugs that limit the richness of our human beingness.

A friend of mine recently addressed this issue playfully in a script about a heavy-drinking opera singer confronting a psychopharmacologist who has promised to cure him:

DOC: Of course, it's difficult to separate, on clinical grounds, true Bi-Polar II from cyclothymic temperamental dysfunction and borderline personality disorders. The point is. You've got a *medical* condition. And I can fix it. I can fix *you*. Like you were a broken vase. We're so good these days, nobody will even notice the crack. Once I'm finished.

SINGER (Pacing, agitated): So let me get this straight. You're telling me that there's something wrong with my head? My brain? You want to operate on me? To fix it?

DOC: No, no. Not operate. Oh. They used to do that, of course. Years ago. A doctor named Freeman. Quite popular. Used an ice pick and a hammer, believe it or not. Of course, I....

SINGER (Overlapping) You're not touching me.

DOC: I see I'm not explaining myself very clearly. Look. What's your range? Starting at C3.

SINGER: Well. Wouldn't want to do it every day. But I once hit a G above high C. So I'm told.

DOC: See! There you have it! Your range is too big. Too low. Too high. Too up and too down. From one pole to another. And your emotional range is like that, too, isn't it?

SINGER: What the hell good would notes be if you didn't have the feelings to go along with them?

DOC: It may seem like that to you now. But you'll have another perspective later. Once I can stabilize the mood swings. Life looks different from middle C.

SINGER: Middle C, is it? Well. It's a nice note to visit. But I wouldn't want to live there.[21]

Chapter Seven:
The Mystery of Flight

Air, encountering a wing, for no apparent reason behaves so generously toward us mere mortals.

Every time I began to get comfortable flying the airplane, she would reach over and cut off the power to the engine: "OK, John, find a field." This was a test. The training involved always being prepared for an emergency landing — constantly observant for a possible field in which to put the plane down. In this particular case, I noticed we had just flown over a rarely used grass strip. "We are turning for Ridgeway," I said. "Whatever," Michelle replied…like, 'I hope you can make it.'

I set up maximum glide speed, executed a standard rate 180-degree turn, made left downwind, base, and final turns and with no power at all glided into a reasonable, if somewhat clumsy and erratic, landing on the grass. At this point in my training, I took comfort from something I'd read, "Any landing one survives is a good landing."

Early in the training we learn that airplanes, even powered ones, can become sailplanes or gliders, given the right airspeed. One of the first airspeeds one has to know by heart is "best glide speed," the speed at which the plane will make the maximum use of altitude without slowing to the point that it stalls (and crashes). Instructors are fond of taking the trainee's power away and commanding, "nail the glide speed"…that is, immediately configure the plane to attain the published "best glide speed."

You might think that this can't be true for heavy jets, which logic suggests are unsuitable for flight in the first place. But you'd be wrong. Not long ago, a big modern jet was misfueled and halfway between the east and west coasts of Canada ran out of fuel at 35,000 feet. That's right, it ran out of gas. The captain set up best glide speed and, with only the most basic of instruments, transformed his jet into a sailplane and glided to a landing at an abandoned air force base. I have pictures of the plane stopping just a few feet from a group of kids who were using the abandoned field for drag racing. No one aboard was injured, and the plane suffered no serious damage. The captain credited his success to the fact that he was a recreational sailplane flyer.

And, yes, I have had occasion to make a sailplane of my Trinidad. It was mid-February in what had been a cold snowy winter. Acting on our yearning for warmth, we loaded shorts, bathing suits, sunscreen, and all that good stuff and took off for a long weekend of sand and sun on St. Simons Island, Georgia. At 8000 feet over the Chesapeake Bay, the engine began major coughing and sputtering. Some hurried and tense scanning of all relevant indicators suggested that the engine-driven fuel pump had failed. I wasn't worried; we have a back-up electric driven fuel pump. I turned it on and restored power.

Being prudent, we informed ATC that we had an emergency, a fuel pump failure, and were returning to Easton, our home field. (When there is an emergency, the captain does not *ask* ATC; he *tells* them. Following old naval rules, the captain is the ultimate authority when it comes to the safety of his ship, crew or passengers).

We turned back toward our airport, but as luck or Murphy's Law would have it, the electric fuel pump began to rapidly overheat and popped the circuit breaker. Not wishing to risk electrical fire (one of the absolutely worst things imaginable), it was "nail the glide speed" time. It was also time to do my best to calm down and attempt to reassure my passenger that the situation was not as dire as it seemed. Nevertheless, it's difficult to ignore the sound of silence when the engine quits! Taking her hand, I said, "I've done this many times as an exercise. Don't worry" (as she tightened her shoulder harness). When we had completed a 180-degree turn, she could see the airport just eight miles ahead, and I could feel her relax. Or maybe I was the one relaxing! At 7000 feet, maintaining precise glide speed that close to the airport was relatively easy, and we made a comfortable enough power-off landing. Still it felt mighty good to be on solid ground again.

It is the altitude that matters. In flying, we are taught that altitude equals energy. But altitude or energy has limits, and managing that limited energy becomes essential to survival.

Managing "altitude" is crucial in our everyday lives as well. Whether we are at 35,000 feet or 3500 feet, we have only a limited amount of energy available. Wasting energy will most certainly limit our gliding range.

Some of us have had the opportunity to witness Bob Hoover, an older stunt pilot, do some amazing feats with his rather large twin-engine airplane, which he calls his "energy management series." He will fly by from right to left at a little above eye level, climb to a decent height, circle while gaining momentum, and return to fly by at eye level right to left. Only this time, before he is in front of us, he has killed both engines and feathered the props. He flies by quietly with just the whoosh of the wind, the props absolutely still. Then he is up into a half-loop, flying back left to right doing an absolutely perfect eight-point roll, a half-loop at the other end, gliding back into a perfect landing, and still with enough momentum to turn from the runway and coast to the very spot from which he departed. It is a tribute to this man that his Shrike Commander is now in the Smithsonian's Air and Space Museum, the new Steven F. Udvar-Hazy Center.

What magnificent lives we could live if we could but learn to manage our personal energy so well.

Yet we waste untold precious energy in conflicts, disagreements, and foolish attempts at control. Although we can squander energy in every arena, we are most profligate in the relationships within which we seek emotional closeness. Enormous energy is expended in quarrels, fights between couples, fights between parents and children. Fighting people end up completely spent and exhausted, unable to do the useful, creative work that requires emotional calm. We see this waste of energy all around, internationally as well as interpersonally. On a global level, the amount of fighting among people is both frightening and tragic.

Susan is a highly organized person, focusing constantly on the things that need to be done around the house and yard. Bill, her husband, is a bit more laid back. He judges that he works hard during the week, and on weekends he feels entitled to relax and play. You know the scene. Susan wastes an enormous amount of energy in her frustrated attempts to make things go in the orderly way she desires. On the other hand, Bill wastes energy by passively-aggressively withdrawing from the whole situation. Weekends are a disaster, leaving both partners depleted and unhappy. They could find relief from their distress if they were they able to relate to each other in terms of their feelings, as discussed earlier. However, more to the point here, we are foolish to waste so much energy in our attempts to over-manage things and people. In flying, we know that our power to control has serious limits, but that truth becomes obscured in our attempts to control others and the multitudinous tasks of our lives.

When Jane came in for her session, a quick glance told me that she had gotten depressed again. She described the classic symptoms, fitful sleep or insomnia, no interest in anything, a complete absence of the sexual desire that she had recently begun to experience anew, barely enough energy to get out of bed. It took a sheer act of will to get her to the appointment. Because we had been working together for some time on issues related to her depression, I said, "OK, Jane, what is it that you are trying so hard not to feel?" After a long silence, she said almost inaudibly, "I think I know." She then added with a stronger voice, "I think it's the shame business that we have dealt with before." She described an incident at work the day before in which her supervisor had accused her of not flushing the toilet after herself. (Trust me that can be a focus for some people!) Jane had been incredibly shamed when growing up, and all of those same old feelings began flooding through her after this incident. As she had done many times before, she mobilized most of her life energy to push these feelings away, a process psychologists call "suppression" or "repression." When we consider the finite nature of our life energy, suppressing feelings is the most egregious way to waste it.

We could speculate that Jane unconsciously set herself up for this experience of shame. We all walk around with suppressed feelings and unconsciously look for occasions to express them. *Our life experiences do not <u>cause</u> us to experience particular feelings so much as they provide opportunities for feelings to which we are especially entitled.* Maybe Jane was unconsciously entitling herself to these feelings of shame, maybe not. It is difficult to know for sure. Indeed, it would be unfair to assume that Jane was guilty as charged with the crime of "not flushing." What happened, however, was not a bad thing; rather it was an *opportunity* for Jane to entitle herself to a much needed expression of feeling.

We say that we *get* depressed as if we are passive victims of something outside ourselves. It is more accurate to say that we *depress ourselves*. Much of what we call depression is an active process by which we take our life energy and employ it to distance ourselves from feelings that we desperately do *not* want to feel. It is no wonder then that the primary symptoms of depression are listlessness, lifelessness, lack of libido, and lack of life energy.

What happened to Jane? She sobbed uncontrollably for some time. She recalled some of her early experiences of shame. However, feelings are transitory, and eventually her shame abated. She left smiling.

I know you must be thinking, it can't be that simple. But it is. Stopping smoking is simple, too. You just stop doing what you have been habitually doing. Of course, *simple* isn't the same thing as *easy*. Breaking habits is incredibly difficult, and that is especially true about patterns of adjustment we have employed to keep unwanted feelings at bay.

Again, the main point is: Using up our precious life energy to keep from feeling the feelings we feel is a very bad strategy. It is like attempting to "stretch the glide" in an airplane.

We are suddenly in a curious situation when the engine quits in flight. Setting up for best glide speed involves an acknowledgement of the Anima and the Animus, the right hemispheric and the left hemispheric experiences of ourselves. We must use our *logos,* our logical thinking to manage what we can manage, and our *eros,* our sensual feelings to determine what the plane needs to continue gliding. Attempting to "stretch the glide" is courting disaster, though pilots sometimes try to do it anyway. Seeing a landing spot he would like to reach — perhaps an airport — even an experienced pilot will occasionally hold back pressure on the yoke, inadvertently slowing the wing to a stall, spin and crash. Most of these accidents are fatal. This is especially unfortunate when a perfectly good field was available for a controlled approach; the type of emergency landing one often walks away from without injury.

We're talking survival skills here. How do we manage the limited life energy available? How do we live in harmony with the air that supports us, that keeps our wing flying?

Even after one hundred years of powered flight, we actually do not know what makes a wing fly. And, of course, what makes a wing fly is absolutely basic to everything that has to do with airplanes. In learning to fly an airplane, one has to pass FAA tests that use the official explanation of how a wing gives lift. As Peter Garrison [1] writes, that explanation goes something like this: Neighboring air molecules that part company at the leading edge, some to pass above the wing and some to pass underneath, must meet at the trailing edge. Since the airfoil is humped and the distance along the upper surface is greater than that along the bottom, it follows that the velocity must be greater along the upper surface. Bernoulli (a Swiss mathematician) is then invoked to demonstrate that higher velocity means lower pressure, and lo and behold we have lift.

Garrison, who writes a regular column in *Flying* magazine, adds: "This explanation, which is at least vaguely familiar even to some persons who have no special interest in flight, rests firmly upon a falsehood that molecules that were neighbors as the wing approached are still neighbors after it has passed. Why should this be true? Indeed, it is not...[experiments] show that the air traveling along the upper surface of the airfoil reaches the trailing edge well in *advance* of that following the lower surface, in spite of having traveled a greater distance...These [experiments], which ought to be in every textbook about aviation, show not only why the pressure on the upper surface is less than on the lower, but also why this should be called 'The Secret of Flight'...*It seems to me that exposure to [these experiments] merely increases one's bafflement, amazement and delight that air, encountering a wing, for no apparent reason behaves so unexpectedly, so helpfully, so generously toward us mere mortals.*" (Italics mine.) [1]

Existentially, it seems appropriate that we stand in awe and wonder at the mysteries of life. Like the air moving across a wing, perhaps there is an Energy of Love and Truth and Goodness and Beauty that, for no apparent reason, behaves unexpectedly, helpfully and generously toward us mere mortals. In flying we clearly must respect this mystery of flight and live in accord with it. That necessary humility provides a powerful lesson for all spheres in which we act.

As someone who for many years has been a resource for people who are trying to overcome estrangement in their relationships, I have learned that passion (Eros) is most likely to erupt in our lives if we first acknowledge and live in harmony with existential mystery. Too little attention is given to establishing a context within which love and respect can spontaneously flourish. We speak of passionate feelings as if we could *will* them to be. But we can't. Thinking that we "should" love someone is entirely a left-hemispheric management approach, and it doesn't work. People stand at the altar and promise to love till they die, as if willing the feeling to last will make it last. Interestingly, people do not generally promise to *like* each other forever. The spontaneous outpouring of loving feelings toward another person requires a context and a mood within which those feelings can arise. This is like configuring a plane for gliding, with an awareness of the mysterious forces that keep a wing in flight and with a clear acknowledgment of the limitation of our power.

Creating an environment within which feelings of respect and love can flourish is especially important in parent-child relationships. From an existential perspective, respect for the other is essential. Yes, it is appropriate for children to respect parents. But that is most likely to happen spontaneously if the parent respects the child first. Meaningful respect is not a technique, a role to play, an act of will. Rather, it is an honoring of the other in his or her essential human beingness. It is taking delight in the child, enjoying the child's individuality of expression, supporting his or her dignity. Why is it so hard to trust that respected children will, in turn, respect their parents?

Most of us have witnessed the opposite kind of parent-child relationship — the out-of-control mother screaming at her out-of-control child in the supermarket — with little respect evident either way. Unfortunately, such scenes tend to replicate themselves from generation to generation. *We tend to relate to others the way we were related to.* Even more importantly, we relate to *ourselves* the way we were related to by the significant others of our past. You see the problem. It is difficult to spontaneously relate to another person with respect if we were not respected when we were children. Moreover, if we were not respected when we were children, it is highly unlikely we will respect ourselves when we become adults.

Because I believe, as Harry Stack Sullivan did, that we are primarily formed in our relationships with significant others, my initial history-taking with a client involves listing all the important people, past and present, in the person's life. I am again and again impressed by the positive effect on personality development when at least one person on the list spontaneously and freely enjoyed the client. Many people have no memory of being related to with such positive delight and pleasure. Making room, or providing a context, for the spontaneous expressions of love, respect, and pleasure with a child is more important than most parents realize.

Incredible amounts of emotional energy are wasted in the authoritarian power struggles between parents and children. In Center City Philadelphia, I once observed a woman dragging her crying child by the hand and screaming, "you *will* go see Santa Claus!" I have often noticed that the strong-willed defiant child usually has an equally strong-willed parent. Such parents can gain a marvelous freedom by identifying with the child's rebellion and seeing it as an expression of personal integrity. With this change in attitude, a feeling of respect spontaneously occurs — often followed by a deeper shift in perspective that makes the old authoritarian way of relating suddenly seem ludicrous.

Our existential "thrownness into human beingness" [2] would seem to lead naturally to a respect for all people. When it doesn't, it is because of distortions in our early relationships. Psychotherapy can help correct these distortions by providing a relationship of great significance and profound respect within which the client can feel truly honored. Like other therapists who have worked with couples, I have often seen partners able to feel more love and respect for each other because they were feeling loved and respected by the therapist. Aligning ourselves with this attitude of love and respect is like configuring a plane for gliding. Some power to control is surrendered as we seek an alignment with a mysterious lift that supports ecstatic soaring.

Air, encountering a wing, for no apparent reason behaves generously toward us. Life is full of mystery; the more we know, the more mystery we discover. Scientists who know most about the composition of the cosmos are humbled by how little they know about what the cosmos is. For hundreds of years, scientists assumed that the study of visible matter was the study of all that exists. Now it seems that some unseeable something-or-other rules the cosmos and that ordinary matter is just along for the ride. Ordinary matter might be only about four percent of whatever-it-is-that-is. Some physicists estimate that about twenty percent of the universe is dark matter, about which we know little; and eighty percent is some kind of energy that we have no good way of measuring. However, as someone once observed, even if dark energy and dark matter ultimately dictate the overall course of cosmic events, ordinary matter has the consolation of expressing the visible life of the universe, softening the brute force of the cosmos like a flower box in the middle of Manhattan. As suggested earlier, I like to picture this mysterious cosmic energy as an Energy of Love and Truth and Goodness and Beauty, an invisible force that provides a lift to our wings, sustaining us in flight. Of course, that is only a picture; but one of our most precious gifts as human beings is our ability to picture beyond our immediate visible field.

When macho management of the invisible forces fails and we contemplate how best to configure our flight, other life mysteries deserve respect as well. I was sitting next to my father one night, in deep philosophical discussion, when he suddenly looked pale and worried. I asked what was wrong. "Oh nothing," he said. "I just felt something had happened to Cy [a close friend living hundreds of miles away]." Nothing more was said, but the next morning, the phone rang and Dad learned that his friend had been in a serious automobile accident at exactly the time when we had had our conversation the night before. Many people have similar experiences but they are reluctant to share them because there is no recognized scientific explanation for such phenomena.

Like other people I know, I have had similar experiences of profound connection with others that defy rational explanation, connections that at times feel visceral. It seems that when we are emotionally attuned with those who are special to us, a communication occurs even over long distances. We sense when something of emotional import is occurring.

This phenomenon no doubt is related to the mysterious energy of the cosmos, and it challenges our too-material focus.

Some people are attempting to ground these somewhat mysterious experiences in empirical science. A physician, Larry Dossey, suggests the concept "nonlocal consciousness" to describe this parapsychological cognition or emotional awareness. Dossey would like to see modern medicine move from "Era I mechanical medicine," based on Newtonian physics, in which all disease was considered to be the result of forces acting locally within individuals; through "Era II mind-body medicine," based on an understanding that emotions, attitudes, and beliefs can act causally to promote health and healing; to "Era III nonlocal medicine," in which how the physician thinks and feels toward the patient, holds the patient in his/her awareness, affects the healing process.[2] This is an interesting concept that might, with time and more study, gain credibility.

Certainly we can hypothesize a connection between energy and healing. Barbara Brennan, whom I know and respect, believes there is a strong relationship between the two. Her focus is on the auric energy field that she believes surrounds the human body, indeed, an energy that exists around all material forms: "I learned to see the energy fields of trees and small animals. I discovered that everything has an energy field around it that looks somewhat like the light from a candle. I also began to notice that everything was connected by these energy fields, that no space existed without an energy field. Everything, including me, was living in a sea of energy." [3]

Barbara has a degree in atmospheric physics and for a number of years did research for NASA. While NASA for most people is associated with space exploration, we pilots know it to be our friend — an organization that promotes General Aviation and works to enhance our safety. NASA sometimes acts as a buffer between the enforcement arm of the FAA to encourage reports of problems between pilots and air traffic controllers when safety is not compromised but improvements can be made.

Indeed it is her scientific background that persuades Barbara that we have seriously limited our self-understanding by grounding our perception in Newtonian physics, insisting on seeing ourselves as solid objects. Modern physics shows that matter does not exist with certainty in definite places, but rather shows "tendencies" to exist. All particles of matter can be created from energy and vanish into energy.

Our too-solid grounding in a purely physical understanding of matter, with little awareness of the multitudinous manifestations of energy, continues to limit our perspective. Einstein's theory of the relativity of matter and energy is proven every day both in the peaceful uses of atomic energy and the destructive potential of nuclear weapons.

Comprehending these subtle but powerful forms of energy manifested around us will likely remain difficult for most of us. Also exaggerated claims of healing powers through one or another kind of energy are troubling to anyone with a rigorous scientific background. As one of my friends says, there are a lot of "wand wavers" around who expect great leaps of faith to support untested and untestable "truths." At the same time, we need an openness to new ways of perceiving reality. Modern physics leads us toward an appreciation of the sea of energy in which we live and move and have our being.

For me, a healthy skepticism is necessary in these matters. After all, to "nail the glidespeed," one has to consult the airspeed indicator. It is a tricky matter, this anima-animus balance. Some pilots can probably "fly by the seat of their pants," especially if in an open-cockpit biplane. Merely by the sound of the wind in the wires and the feel of the plane, they can establish the correct glide speed with no reference to instruments. Me? I welcome the technology of the simple, reliable airspeed indicator if I am to establish harmony with the mysterious energy that provides lift to my wing. This instrument has a little tube under the wing to measure passage of air; and in addition to checking the engine oil and other things, my preflight inspection always involves checking that "pitot tube." I make certain that no little critters are blocking the opening.

Enjoy the mystery of flight, but check the pitot tube.

I have made this an existential mantra to support my skepticism about any "truths" requiring great leaps of faith.

Yet I try to maintain an open stance toward anything unusual that might help in our psychological life processes. Not too long ago, I seriously frightened myself (embraced some anxiety) by signing up for a weekend of exorcism or "soul retrieval." The workshop was being led by a teacher of Shamanistic healing on the faculty of Barbara Brennan's academy. I knew I was in trouble when the instructions arrived saying I should bring a portable massage table, drums and feathers. I found drums. Some years ago, I had traded my binoculars for drums with a Tarahumara Indian boy in the Copper Canyon of Chihuahua. However, I was without table, feathers or confidence that I was in my right mind.

To my surprise, the experience proved enlightening. The heart of the process involved giving loving support to people as they relived objectionable experiences of great emotional import in their lives. There was much screaming and crying and gnashing of teeth. Or sometimes more quiet but deep sobbing. All of this expression of feeling was contained in a hands-on atmosphere of nonjudgmental support. It was easy to observe the transformation from visible tension and conflict to faces that were open, relaxed and with a definite healthy appearance. After being a novice giver and a receiver in this process, I was told by a friend that she had never seen me looking so radiant.

Impressed, I said to Jane, "this does not seem dissimilar to my work, but much more expeditious. It takes me years to help people get to this place." She responded: "John, when you get people to that place of wholeness they have integrated these experiences. These dear ones have had the experience, but it will take years to integrate it all. We both get to the same place at the same time." Jane's comment was comforting and is perhaps correct about the psychic economy of such emotional expression.

Accepting the possibility that we live and move and have our being in a sea of mystery whose nature we do not fully understand means relinquishing rigid commitment to old paradigms. This is a bit like configuring the airplane for gliding. There is considerable discomfort when the engine quits and we must relinquish the safe assumption of how we are going to get from point A to point B. Our assumptions about our lives can be like that. Perhaps in our determination to manage everything in life we have pushed down so much feeling that we have lost our souls and they can be retrieved only if we embrace the "demons." In flying, we sometimes have to surrender to the fact that we no longer have the power to make the plane go wherever we want. We have to accept that she will glide, and glide very well, if we pay attention to what she needs to stay aloft on the ambient energy. This gliding can mean surrendering to some powerful updrafts and downdrafts of air, demons over which one has no control.

At other less troubled times, experiencing the thrust of a powerful engine can feel Animus, quite "male." When the engine stops, surrendering to the feel of the plane, listening to what sounds right with the wind across her wing, can feel Anima, comfortably "female." There is macho sense of strength in feeling the power of an engine, but there is something approaching ecstasy in gliding through the air in this magical feeling way.

Jung writes, "the anima and the animus live in a world quite different from our own; in a world where the pulse of time beats ever so slowly; where the birth and death of individuals count little, and where ten thousand years ago is yesterday." [4]

When the aircraft is gliding, we encounter the true wonder and mystery of flying, an experience that brings to mind Jung's belief in the inherent mystery of the Anima. Clearly, being in harmony with whatever-it-is-that-is enables us to fly. Being in harmony with whatever-it-is-that-is enables us to live. As Peter Garrison has observed, there is amazement and delight that air, encountering a wing, for no apparent reason behaves so unexpectedly, so helpfully, so generously toward us mere mortals. Our capacity for amazement, delight, and generosity comes toward us out of an equally mysterious realm of energy. Perhaps in the not too distant future people will look back at us amazed that we knew so much about matter and so little about energy. After all, people once believed the earth was flat.

The fact that we might not fully understand what makes an airplane fly does not prevent us from enjoying the benefits of flying. Similarly, the fact that we might not fully understand the energy that sustains us in life does not prevent us from enjoying ourselves and each other and the beauty of creation. In the human realm, reliance on power alone can have dreadful consequences. In our personal lives, or in a wider social context, power can fail; and without the ability to attune ourselves to the underlying energy of love and beauty supporting us, we can quickly spin out of control into a world of ugliness and hate, just as an airplane can spin out of control and crash when it loses lift to her wing.

On the other hand, acknowledging the limits of macho power and striving for a harmony with this mysterious and generous Energy that provides lift, results in a most precious experience in which Love and Beauty come rushing up to meet us.

Chapter Eight:
The Rescue

Ontologically, beauty is the secret sound
of the deepest thereness of things.

The call came at a little after 7 a.m. "John, we need your help. A baby harbor seal has washed ashore at Virginia Beach. If we do not get her to the Aquarium today, she will die. Are you available?" "Sure, Dave. I'll clear my calendar. I'll meet you at the General Aviation Ramp at BWI at 8:30."

I was flying this mission for the Environmental Air Force. The EAF is an organization of pilots who volunteer to do things such as fly photographers to out-of-the-way sites. I once flew photographers for the Nature Conservancy to an island on the upper Delaware River being considered for purchase and another time to photograph an area where someone was poaching trees on Conservancy property. However, most of my missions have been for the Baltimore Aquarium. The biologists are glad to have me fly them around the Chesapeake Bay to do their marine mammal surveys. They tell me they can accomplish in two hours what it would take two weeks to do in a boat.

It was my connection with the Baltimore Aquarium that involved me in this seal rescue mission. At BWI, I picked up David Schofield, a marine biologist, and we headed for Virginia Beach. On the way Dave said, "Now, John, sometimes these seals can smell pretty strong. On the beach the smell has brought tears to my eyes." I thought, my God, what have I gotten myself into? Will I even be able to fly this plane with that much distraction? Will the plane ever smell the same?"

The flight to Virginia Beach was otherwise uneventful. We landed and were met by a crew in a station wagon with a dog carrier. Inside was the most beautiful baby seal with the softest, most penetrating large eyes I'd ever seen. It was love at first sight. Besides, she did not smell that bad — a bit like a wet dog.

As we placed her on the back seat of the plane, Dave informed me, "Now, John, we probably should not go up very high with her. I don't know what altitude will do, but I'll sit back here with her and monitor her vital signs."

In filing my flight plan back to BWI, I had told ATC that we were transporting a live harbor seal for the EAF and shouldn't fly over 4000 feet (an arbitrary number, but we need at least that much altitude over Norfolk's air space). In flight, the Norfolk controller, in an excited voice, replied: "Zero, Foxtrot, Quebec, we have to get you up to 5000 feet momentarily — we have a jet coming toward you at 4000." "Wilco, Foxtrot Quebec." The next controller was Richmond. A female voice said, "We're getting you right back down to four." We were cleared through Patuxant Naval Air Station, through Andrews Air Force Base and into BWI with our precious cargo. There we were met by the Aquarium's rescue van and a TV crew.

The happy conclusion to this tale is that our seal survived and is thriving in her new home. Beauty comes to us in many unexpected ways.

O'Donohue writes, "Ontologically, beauty is the secret sound of the deepest thereness of things. To recognize and celebrate beauty is to recognize the ultimate sacredness of experience, to glimpse the subtle embrace of belonging where we are wed to the divine, the beauty of every moment, of every thing." [1]

So, you might say, what is the big deal about saving one seal? Maybe it is no big deal; but then, what *is* a big deal? James Serpell of the University of Pennsylvania is one of the new anthrozoologists who believes that in recent centuries we humans have built increased distance between ourselves and the rest of life. Now the great wild world never glances our way. However, people who experience the friendly Orca whale of Nootka Sound, Vancouver, report that when he looks them in the eye they can hardly breathe. [2] Serpell says such experiences make us rethink our whole relationship with animals. I can attest to the fact that it can be that way with a baby harbor seal.

Dan Dagget, an environmentalist, observed "when scientists set out to discover the smallest, most basic form of matter, they encountered particles that were smaller and smaller and smaller, until finally they came to a point where there were no particles at all — no 'things.' There were only relationships. In the most basic sense, then, we don't live in a world of things. We live in a world of relationships." [3] It is clear to me that our denial of our intimate relationship with all that exists is the seedbed for all the ugliness we see. I will talk more in this chapter about the opposite of this intimacy which is a sense of estrangement, a feeling of disconnection and distance that lead to awful exploitation and hatred in human relationships.

At the other end of the spectrum, flying low and slow in itself provides a feeling of respect for our relationship with the earth, sky and water, an experience that can also take one's breath away for the sheer wonder of it. The frightening moments in these flying stories don't do justice to the hundreds of hours of pure enjoyment in having such a wonderful platform from which to observe the beauty of this world.

What we see is not always beautiful, however. Sometimes we see sheer ugliness. I mentioned earlier an experience of flying over West Virginia in the wintertime, when the landscape was dramatic and blissfully serene. On other occasions flying over West Virginia, I have seen sights so ugly I want to cry. We Americans now have the technology to build gigantic machines that literally cut the tops off mountains. This secretive and permanent scaring of the landscape takes place where roads are hidden behind trees that obscure the driver's view. Wendell Berry, another respected environmentalist, commented that no war, so far, has done such extensive or such permanent damage as this destruction of entire mountains. (4)

Huge conduits lead from these open wounds to coal-fired generators, which spew black pollution high into the air. I have hiked trails along the Appalachian Mountains where I've not been able to find a single healthy leaf on a tree. The trees along these mountain ridges are dying from an overload of toxic air. Downwind in the Eastern United States, there is a dramatic rise in asthma and other lung-related diseases.

The exploitative individuals and energy companies responsible for this desecration demonstrate the ugliness of which human beings are capable. How can we justify exploitation? More importantly, how can we justify exploitation of other human beings?

What do we know philosophically without an act of faith or *a priori* assumptions? Heidegger (5) says that what we know for sure is our experience of *throwness into being*. By that, Heidegger asserts that the one choice for certain we did *not* make is the choice *to be*. We experience ourselves in a unique "human beingness" (*Dasein*), living among others who also have this unique human beingness. Authentic relating means relating with that awareness and not treating other human beings as objects to be manipulated or used for our selfish purposes.

We don't need all of the conflicting, confusing rules and regulations of various religions to understand the heart of the matter. We know when we are using others, and we know when we are being used. This intuitive knowledge is a much clearer and more powerful guide than the abstract concept of "conscience."

Psychology would do well to anchor its ethics in the existential understanding that any exploitation of another, any use of another person or treatment of another human being as a "thing at hand" (*Vorhandenheit*), is essentially a denial of both the other's human beingness and one's own. We diminish ourselves when we diminish the other.

There are individuals who do terrible things to others and suffer no pangs of conscience whatsoever. We diagnose these people as sociopathic or, in more extreme cases, psychopathic. The common denominator is an absence of guilt when there ought to be guilt. However, sociopaths are relatively rare. Most of the work in psychotherapy involves helping good people overcome the neurotic guilt produced by an overly critical conscience.

We are all sociopaths sometimes, I suspect. It is difficult to relate to others with such constant authenticity that we never engage in even a subtle manipulation. Without doubt, collectively, socially, we are sociopaths. Men should feel guilt about the privilege of preferential treatment at the expense of women. It is rare to see much of that guilt, however. Those of us in economically developed countries should feel guilt about the exploitation of less economically developed countries that help support our standard of living. It is rare to see much of that guilt either.

Even one's resentment at being used can be obscured. If conscience were a reliable guide, feeling resentful would be a sign that we are giving away too much, that we are accommodating too much, that we are not being fair to ourselves, that we have lost touch with our own human beingness. We have no diagnostic category for being generous to a fault. Timothy Leary (before he blew his mind on LSD) is the only person I know of who attempted to describe and work with this polarity — the polarity between being too selfish and being too generous. It is difficult to make the two extremes sound equally bad. Generally, it seems worse to allow ourselves to exploit others than to allow ourselves to be exploited.

Much of psychotherapy is concerned with what has been called "neurotic guilt," meaning guilt one should not be feeling. Again, however, the standards for this judgment are a bit vague. If our science of the soul were grounded in existential awareness, there would be no vagueness. The only "real" guilt should arise from exploiting others.

When I was a young man, I had a dreadful experience that propelled me from the study of theoretical physics and philosophy into the study of the soul. Friends of our family asked me to speak with their teenage son because he seemed greatly troubled. He had recently joined a fundamentalist religious sect, much to the dismay of his parents. After speaking with him on several occasions, I decided that much of his turmoil had to do with feelings of guilt about masturbation. Because he had begun talking about suicide, I encouraged the family to consult with a psychiatrist. I have no way of knowing what happened in that one consultation, and I assign no blame to the therapist. However, his guilt about masturbation was apparently not assuaged. He returned home and killed himself that same night.

Sexual feelings are part of being human, and much needless suffering could be avoided if we simply accepted that fact. Again, if the psychology of the soul were imbued with existential awareness, the only issue in the expression of sexuality would merely be whether or not it was exploitative. Wouldn't that be a wonderful world! We would embrace our human creativity and variety, and much of what is seen as "deviant" sexuality would lose the weight of judgment. There is no question but that sexual expression can on the one hand be disgustingly ugly and on the other hand be incredibly beautiful.

There are no rules in existentialism, no lists of *shoulds* and *should-nots* to guide moral behavior. Shoulds and should-nots are not derived from our essential human beingness; they are self-serving judgments from those in power who wish to dominate and control others. Transcending the authoritarian milieu from which these multitudes of rules derive is not easy, and it takes courage to live an ethic based solely on valuing, respecting and honoring ourselves and other people.

But there are payoffs. Sexual expression, for example, can be wonderful when it has these qualities.

While driving in Ireland, my friend became hopelessly lost in the town of Limerick. At an intersection, with traffic at a standstill, he lowered his window to inquire of a man who appeared to be local to the area, "Could you tell me how to get to Dingle?" After seeming to give the matter much thought, the man replied, "If I was going to Dingle, I would not be starting from here." It is difficult, if not impossible, to get to the meaningful and satisfying closeness we desire with others from the usual starting point of moral rules. Relationally, there seems to be a high correlation between following the rules and becoming depressed.

One of the most widely accepted but most deadly rules is the Rule of Relational Commitment. The problem is that we can commit behavior, but we cannot by act of will commit feelings, and feelings are the essence of meaningful closeness. If I wanted to get to an exciting and intimate experience, I would not start with behavioral commitments.

George is entirely committed to Ellen and has been for years. He follows the rules, is faithful and proud of it. However, the feeling tone of the household is utter depression. After work, where George is a trusted and valued employee, it is feet up in the recliner and watch TV time. Partly due to low libido, George lost affectional and sexual interest in Ellen years ago. Sometimes Ellen reacts to not being desired by being critical and insulting. George, being a "good" person, does not fight back — openly. But he has been known to refuse to come to the dinner table, especially if Ellen has labored long in cooking something special, a sure sign of his anger in passive-aggressive form. The relationship has become downright ugly. They are committed to each other but are in serious need of rescue.

From an existential standpoint "marriage" is a myth, albeit not necessarily a bad myth, since one of the qualities of a myth is a tapestry upon which we project our desires and longings. The problem is that investment in the myth can disguise the only real truth: What *exists* in a marriage is two people relating and how they relate is of utmost significance. Even being in a relationship can somehow allow people to treat each other in an inauthentic and sometimes exploitative fashion that neither would tolerate if they were not "in a relationship."

Existentially, every relationship is unique and must be judged on an individual basis. The only valid criteria for such a judgment is authenticity and respect; no other rules apply. Let's take a look at several examples of this principal in action.

First, while there are numerous examples of atrocious ways that people relate in marriages, there are also beautiful examples of truly authentic relating that are not under the "holy umbrella."

Janet and Victor have been relating to each other for years. Their connection began with an ancient recognition of belonging, to paraphrase my friend O'Donohue. What they experience in one another's presence is increased aliveness, an intensity of passion and freedom that for them is otherwise rare. The primary qualities of their intimacy are trust and openness; they share more with each other than with anyone else in the world. If one were to paint an idyllic picture of love and friendship, Janet and Victor would be good models.

Here is the dilemma. Victor is formally married to another woman. Periodically he gives himself permission to come alive with Janet, and periodically he goes into panic at the prospect that he might have to define his life in a new way. To make such a choice threatens the security of his established order. In addition he is concerned about how others might judge him. Therefore he has enormous difficulty sustaining the anxiety provoked by his periods of free-flowing aliveness. When he becomes anxious, he pulls back for all he is worth. Janet experiences him as becoming dead and cold. To make matters worse, he says he is leaving her because it is the right thing for *her.*

To return to a previous image: The plane is not under control. It has entered a spin. Pulling back on the yoke has a very predictable result: it tightens the spin and crashes the plane into the rocks and trees below. Victor's pulling back has the same predictable result. He plummets into deadness, lifelessness, and becomes seriously depressed. Ironically, no matter how unhealthy and inauthentic his choice, many will judge that he is "doing the right thing" when he estranges himself from Janet.

In "Upset Recovery" (Chapter Four), I said that a pilot learns to ignore Heading. Attempting to keep a plane on the heading we had predetermined to fly can become the best way to tear the wings off. Yet in life, I see countless people willing to take that risk. Instead of seeking to accommodate the powerful emotional forces that could take them aloft, they plow straight ahead on an inalterable course, making decisions in an unbalanced Animus "male" fashion. In the process, they surrender the precious freedom to choose the only life they have to live.

Sam and Rebecca represent another common relational dilemma. Their marriage has gone flat. Most of Rebecca's energy has been poured into helping her grown children with the problems they are facing. The rest of her energy goes into managing things, which she does very well — her business, her house, and on rare occasions, Sam. Sam does well in his profession; but when he can be, he is a laid-back kind of guy. He enjoys life and has a playful personality. When Sam and Rebecca grew distant, Sam became involved with another woman. His relationship with Susan was stimulating and revitalizing; but, not being given to womanizing, he became troubled by his dual loyalties. He had to make a choice: Either leave Rebecca and make a new life with Susan, or end relating with Susan and try to recover a life with Rebecca toward whom he still felt a deep love and caring. Sam valued living authentically and had no desire to harbor secrets.

Sam's choice was to be open with Rebecca about Susan. As you can imagine, all hell broke loose. Understandably, Rebecca expressed intense hurt and feelings of betrayal. Having developed a trusting relationship with a therapist, Rebecca and Sam hired him as a kind of live-in coach for a series of concentrated sessions. Rebecca and Sam had keen awareness of their feelings and a history of showing some vulnerability when expressing them. Sam was able to empathetically cry with her in full support of her emotional expression, but there was much more. Rebecca had grown up with painful experiences of being shamed. Sam's "affair" elicited an almost overwhelming recurrence of those earlier feelings of shame. After a long and painful process, Rebecca managed to arrive at a place where she could feel truly understood in the expression of her intense feelings. Sam was patient and caring and completely present throughout the therapeutic process, and in an unexpected moment Rebecca completely relaxed and opened herself to him.

At this point the focus shifted to Sam's feelings. He talked about the loss he felt in not experiencing any fun or playfulness with Rebecca. He cried and expressed the helplessness and frustration he had experienced in not being able to entice Rebecca into more relaxed and intimate ways of being together. He made clear that he was not asking Rebecca to excuse his behavior or absolve him. He agreed that there were much better ways for him to have expressed his unhappiness. Rebecca was quick to say that she understood. She was not sure about forgiving him, but she was aware that she had not been present and available to him. She even smiled and said, "I love all that sexuality about you and I miss your playfulness. I want your help in getting that back into our lives." The short ending: They did.

Something ugly had been transformed into something beautiful.

Given all of life's possibilities and an existential awareness that we have choices, should every marriage be saved? Many believe so, and their insistence often results in couples feeling doomed to live in awful estrangement. As we have seen, the stakes are high; the opposite of living a full, exciting life is to live in lethargy and depression. Saving people is a higher priority than saving marriages. It's always satisfying to observe couples overcome estrangement and to see them achieve exciting closeness. I find it equally satisfying to observe a human being break from a "committed relationship" that has become debilitatingly inauthentic, where only the form remains. Again, we might reflect on what we experience as ugly and what we experience as beautiful. "Ontologically, beauty is the secret sound of the deepest thereness of things."

Committing ourselves has its place. We need to be reliable in our promises about what we will do or not do. Nevertheless, behavioral commitments in relationships can be disastrous when feelings are ignored, as when one partner holds the other to a behavioral commitment long after the feelings are gone.

Anne and Carol have lived in a committed relationship for several years. For the past eighteen months the relationship has become distant and difficult, marked by quarreling over petty things, such as whose cat belongs to whom. Sexual relating is practically nonexistent, except when Carol agrees to behave toward Anne in a way that Anne demands. (Anyone who experiences a partner performing sex from duty knows the limited satisfaction in that!)

We observed earlier in the chapter "Hearing Voices" that behavior contrary to feelings can drive any of us crazy. While it would be quite foolish to permanently dissolve a relationship over a momentary feeling shift, attention to a developing absence of emotional bonding is more than prudent. After much soul searching, Carol had come to see that her relationship with Anne was far too containing. She felt blocked in pursuing avenues important for her own growth and development. Although she and Anne had begun with much in common, they had now grown apart. It was not that Anne viewed the crises any differently; as she put it, she came from people who honored their commitments. To this she added a punch line: people choosing same-sex relating should set a good example in doing so.

What Anne was missing is the fundamental existential truth that we can commit behavior, but we cannot commit feelings. The only thing we can do about this fact is to learn to enjoy the moving medium in which we exist. We need to respect her — this Anima soul of our existence — and our choices have to take her into consideration. We also need to respect the Animus rational side from which we evaluate and measure our commitments. It is a trick that requires constant practice, this Anima/Animus balancing act.

Some people seem to think they have all the answers, not only for themselves but also for everyone else. My first philosophy professor had a wonderful saying: It is better to live with a few good questions than to live with a whole host of bad answers. Who can be so certain about abstract right and wrong to know what choices a person should make when faced with life-defining decisions? We need to be rescued from the tyranny of moralistic rules that obscure the complexity of human relationships and often make the experience terribly ugly. A *good* ethical question is: "In the behavioral situation in which I find myself, what is the life-affirming, healthy choice — the choice that embraces both my partner and me in a spontaneous outpouring of love? What choice has the quality of profound respect?"

Kenneth is still feeling troubled by a choice he made to end his brief marriage, a marriage concluded quite amicably and with mutual acknowledgement that it was simply not working. Many young marriages begin as a symbiotic union between two undeveloped souls searching for completion in the other person. We even have conventional phrases for this symbiosis — "the two becoming one" or references to "my better half." While we likely can't change something so basic as this human tendency toward symbiotic attachment, we need to be rescued from a blindness that does not allow for human growth. The process of becoming more mature and more whole as an individual can play havoc with symbiotic choices. From their symbiotic beginnings, Kenneth and his wife Evelyn had each grown as individuals and were staring into the face of incompatible and irreconcilable lifestyles and expectations. Their only healthy choice was to give up the incessant fights focused on changing the other person and to go their separate ways.

However, Kenneth was still ruminating about his choice, wondering whether he had done the "right" thing. His mother had added a note of heaviness, "but we have never had a divorce in our family!" Like

Kenneth, we also need rescue from the obligation to conform to the expectations of others and to obey abstract moral rules. With some young childless couples, I have sometimes suggested picturing forming a relationship as one might sculpt a work of art from clay. Sometimes the clay we have chosen is highly malleable and we form something very beautiful. Sometimes the chosen clay is workable for a while but then begins to harden and crumble, and we are unable to get it to hold together to form the shape we desire. That is disappointing if we had invested considerable time and energy in the process. The outcome does not constitute a mistake, however. This is simply part of an ongoing process of living truthfully and authentically. Kenneth seemed somewhat intrigued with the image and broke into a huge smile when I asked, "if you were a sculptor would you give up just because your first statute did not work out to your satisfaction?"

By virtue of being human, we have choices. Existentially, denial of choice is the source of all inauthenticity. Denial of choice in relationships inevitably leads to form without substance. We need rescuing from the still prevalent view that once we are married or in a "committed" relationship, our choices go out the window. *There can be no authentic relating without the choice to not relate.* In truth, many married couples only infrequently choose to relate to each other. They spend most of their energy on finding ways *not* to relate. Because these choices to not relate are seldom "owned" or acknowledged, the actual relating is entirely inauthentic. In many cases, the healthy move for the relationship might be to "end the relationship." Free of formal commitment, the partners might be able to experience themselves as living, authentic, self-determining beings, *choosing* to relate to each other with renewed enthusiasm, having together something beautiful.

Jim called Joan a "fucking bitch." She took off her ring and threw it across the room screaming, "you ignorant bastard." He took off his ring and threw it back. They were soon to be married and had promised when they exchanged these rings never to remove them. They had also agreed never to use this language when speaking to each other. "It sounds as if you ended your relationship," I said. There was a long pause, then both agreed it felt that way. "Well, that's good. It seems to me most of the time when people talk about ending a relationship, they really just want to choose to end the way they are relating. Sounds like a reasonable choice." They both agreed. The fight was the result of assuming that what they were feeling did not matter. When they began to relate again with an inviting sensitivity to each other's feelings, they had a wonderful time becoming close. This authentic moving apart and moving back is seldom given the honor it deserves.

Too much regard for one's security can also destroy authentic relating. If a marriage is defined as a "mutual security pact," awareness of choice can become obscured and the vital, exciting, dynamic way the two people had been relating can disappear overnight. I had friends who, after ten or twelve years of "free associating," decided to get married. At the wedding I remarked, "I hope what is done here today does not ruin this fabulous relationship." The place broke up with spontaneous applause. Somewhere within we know that the external structure of marriage can sometimes serve to extinguish the spontaneous delight and genuine pleasure two people can enjoy in each other's company.

Intimate relationships can be incredibly satisfying and beautiful; consequently the possibilities for hurt and disappointment often seem worth the risk. Existentially, a human being in isolation is a contradiction in terms. Sure, we can survive all by ourselves, but not too happily. To experience the fullness of our human beingness, we require emotional closeness with others. As John O'Donohue says, "The call of Eros is at the heart of the human person. Although each of us is fashioned in careful incompletion, we were created to long for each other." [6]

After years of attempting to be a resource for troubled people in troubled relationships, I believe we are all in need of rescue — rescue from the tyranny of too many rules, from exhaustion in seeking false security, from an unbalanced controlling stance... in short, rescue from everything that keeps life from unfolding and flowering as it might in beautiful human closeness.

Existentially, there is for me one basic truth: If we have not established relationships with others whom we trust implicitly and with whom we can be completely open, if there is no one who provokes spontaneous feelings of love and wonder and in whose presence we abandon all our defenses in unguarded intimacy — then we have missed out on the greatest privilege of our human beingness. [7]

Postscript

A harbor seal breaths air, needs the water, and uses the land. All are necessary for survival. And since one-third of the earth's surface is land, two thirds is covered by water and three-thirds is covered by air, all are necessary for the survival of our human beingness.

We know that human beings are the real danger to the earth, the water, the air. And human beings are the real danger to other human beings. We know it. We feel it. The anxiety is palpable.

Psychologists rightfully have been accused of ignoring these big problems and this wider social dis-ease in a too-narrow focus with individuals and couples. It is a bit like fiddling while Rome burns.

I believe it is important to observe that much of the acute anxiety of our day comes from an intuitive awareness that the air we breathe, the water we drink and the land we inhabit are becoming increasingly polluted and that pollution threatens our continued existence. Nor can we obscure the fact that mobility and technology have dramatically increased the potential devastation human beings might cause, not only acting collectively as national states but simply as individuals dedicated to killing and maiming. The resulting fear and helplessness can create a reaction among us that plunges the human world scene into ever increasing and widespread ugliness and hate.

As in the interaction in a marriage, reactive anger and aggression can cause a defensive and aggressive response. Predictably, the result is an irrational attempt to destroy the threat, in almost every case a potential human partner.

Freud had an understanding of the phenomenon of projection in which human beings soon become very much like those that they hate. Depth psychology thus provides much needed insight into the dynamics of human estrangement. "It takes only a bit of perspective to observe that the values and orientation of ourselves and our enemies become increasingly indistinguishable. We can easily disguise the ways that Christian and Muslim fundamentalists have much in common, and the compelling resemblance that violence bears to violence, whether it is termed terrorism or the war on terror." [1]

On a global scale we are in dire need of these psychological insights because in the religious, ethnic and political struggles of our day, we have lost our way. What are the specific solutions? I don't know. Psychotherapy is not about telling people what to do. It is about providing insight — insight and understanding so that we can make conscious and creative choices, choices that respect both ourselves and others, choices that free us from reactive, hateful violence. We need a psychology dedicated to providing this insight and a psychology imbued with enough existential philosophy to support some truly risky, creative solutions.

Notes

TITLE PAGE

(1) O'Donohue, *Anam Cara*, p.95.
(2) Ibid. p.88.

FRONTISPIECE

(1) Paz, Octavio, *Eagle or Sun*, p.25. Original in paragraph form. Blank verse arrangement is my choice.

CHAPTER ONE

(1) Jung, Carl, *The Integration of the Personality*, p.11.
(2) Tillich, Paul, *The Courage To Be*, p.38.
(3) Sullivan, Harry Stack, *Collected Works*. Vol. II, Part I.
(4) *Anam Cara*.
(5) Kierkegaard, Soren, *The Sickness Unto Death*, p.167.

CHAPTER TWO

(1) *Anam Cara*, p151.

(2) Jung, Carl, *Man and His Symbols*, p.61.

(3) Ibid. p.60.

(4) Miller, Jean Baker, *Toward a New Psychology of Women*, p.29.

(5) Salih, Sara, *The Judith Butler Reader*, p.26.

(6) Campbell, Joseph, Ed., *The Portable Jung*, p.151. Jung also wrote, "The animus corresponds to the paternal logos, just as the anima corresponds to the maternal Eros. In men, Eros, the function of relationship, is usually less developed than Logos. In women, on the other hand, Eros is an expression of their true nature, while their Logos is often a regrettable accident." p.152.

(7) Hyde, Janet Shibley, "The Gender Similarities Hypothesis," *American Psychologist, Sept. 2005, pp. 581-592.*

(8) *Anam Cara*, p.186.

CHAPTER THREE

(1) De Saint-Exupery, Antoine, *Wind, Sand and Stars,* p.3.

(2) Ibid. p.20.

(3) Sasz, Thomas, *The Myth of Mental Illness.*

(4) Interestingly, this heightened "interpersonal sensitivity" has become one of the defining symptoms of Bipolar Disorder! *Journal of Affective Disorders*, Jan. 2003, pp.87-98.

CHAPTER FOUR

(1) Currently, the word "animus" is used sometimes to define pent-up anger or aggression, as in "that group has an animus toward us." For Jung this usage would imply a narrow and negative view of the *Animus.*

(2) Sullivan, Harry Stack, *The Interpersonal Theory of Psychiatry.*

CHAPTER FIVE

[1] Tavris, p.121.

[2] Sullivan, op.cit.

[3] Maslow, Abraham, *Toward A Psychology Of Being*, pp.191-192.

[4] Eisler, Riane, *The Chalice and The Blade*, p.xviii.

[5] *Psychology Today*, 1988.

[6] Eisler, op.cit.

[7] Ibid.

[8] Seabrook, Paul, *The Company of Strangers*, quoted in *The Economist*, August 14, 2004.

CHAPTER SIX

[1] Harwi, Anne Davy

[2] *Anam Cara*.

[3] Jung, *Integration*, p.11.

[4] *Scientific American*, Vol.290, No.5, p.85.

[5] *National Psychologist*, March/April, 2004, p13.

[6] Jamison, p.204.

[7] Ibid. p.165.

[8] Ibid. p.203.

[9] Blake, William, "Auguries of Innocence."

[10] Coulehan, Jack, "Chekhov's Doctors," *Uncharted Lines*, p.19.

[11] *Scientific American*, op.cit., p88, italics mine.

[12] Sasz, op.cit., p.205.

[13] *Anam Cara*.

[14] Coulehan, op. cit., p.20.

[15] Harwi, Anne Davy

[16] *Anam Cara*, pp.235-236.

[17] Woolf, p.225.

[18] Quoted by Jamison, op.cit., p.237.

[19] Perhaps because this wording is unusual it becomes an effective way of thinking about and expressing this phenomenon.

[20] De Saint-Exupery, op,cit., p.49.

[21] Steffen-Fluhr, Nancy, "Heartbreaker," Copyright February 2004.

CHAPTER SEVEN

[1] Garrison, Peter, *Flying*, Vol. 129, No.7, p.99.

[2] Dossey, Larry, "Science Within Consciousness," Vol.2, No.1, pp.2-3.

[3] Brennan, Barbara, *Hands of Light*, p.5.

[4] Jung, *Integration*, p.25.

CHAPTER EIGHT

[1] O'Donohue, *Beauty*, p.51.

[2] See *Smithsonian*, vol.35, no.8, pp.64-71.

[3] See *Orion*, vol.23, no.6, p.7.

[4] Ibid. p.21.

[5] Heidegger, Martin, *Being and Time*. Heidegger, the philosopher, must be distinguished from Heidegger, the man, called by one commentator, a German redneck. Unfortunately, he never quite separated himself from the German nationalism of his time, yet his philosophy has remained deeply influential on many who certainly have not shared his politics.

[6] *Beauty*, p.153.

[7] Similar to a sentiment expressed by Alan Dewitt Button in *The Authentic Child*, a book I have recommended

Bibliography of Works Cited

Breedlove, Charlene, Ed. *Uncharted Lines: Poems from the Journal of the American Medical Association.* Albany CA: Boaz Publishing Co., 1998.

Brennan, Barbara Ann. *Hands of Light: A Guide to Healing Through the Human Energy Field.* New York: Bantam Books, 1987.

Brennan, Barbara Ann. *Light Emerging: The Journey of Personal Healing.* New York: Bantam Books, 1993.

Button, Alan DeWitt. *The Authentic Child.* New York: Random House, 1969.

Campbell, Joseph. *The Portable Jung.* New York: The Viking Press, 1971.

Chapman, A. H. *Harry Stack Sullivan: The Man and His Work.* New York: G.P. Putnam's Sons, 1976.

De Saint-Exupery, Antoine. *Wind, Sand and Stars.* New York: Harcourt Brace & Company, 1939.

Eisler, Riane. *The Chalice and the Blade: Our History, Our Future.* San Francisco: Harper Collins, 1987.

Heidegger, Martin. *Being and Time.* Trans. J. Macquarrie and E. Robinson. San Francisco: Harper Collins, 1962.

Jamison, Kay Redfield. *Touched With Fire: Manic-Depressive Illness and the Artistic Temperament*. New York: Simon and Schuster, 1993.

Jung, Carl G. *The Integration of the Personality*. Trans.S. Dell. New York: Farrar & Rinehart, Inc., 1939.

Jung, Carl G. *Man and His Symbols*. New York: Doubleday & Co., 1964.

Kierkegaard, Soren. *Concluding Unscientific Postscript*. Princeton: Princeton Univ. Press, 1944.

Kierkegaard, Soren. *Purity of Heart is to Will One Thing*. Trans. D. Steere. New York: Harper Torchbooks, 1956.

Maslow, Abraham H. *Toward a Psychology of Being*. New York: John Wiley & Sons, Inc., 1999.

Miller, Jean Baker. *Toward a New Psychology of Women*. 2nd ed. New York: Beacon Press, 1986.

O'Donohue, John. *Anam Cara: A Book of Celtic Wisdom*. New York: Harper Collins, 1997.

O'Donohue, John. *Divine Beauty: The Invisible Embrace*. New York: Bantam Press, 2003.

Paz, Octavio. *Eagle or Sun*. New York: New Directions Publishing Corp., 1969.

Salih, Sara, Ed. *The Judith Butler Reader*. Malden, MA: Blackwell Publishing, 2004.

Sasz, Thomas S. *The Myth of Mental Illness*. New York: Paul B. Hoeber, Inc., 1961.

Sullivan, Harry Stack. *The Collected Works of Harry Stack Sullivan*, 2 Vols. Eds. H. Perry and M. Gawel. New York: W.W. Norton & Co., Inc., 1953.

Tavris, Carol. *Anger: The Misunderstood Emotion*. New York: Simon and Schuste, 1982.

Tillich, Paul. *The Courage to Be.* New Haven: Yale University Press, 1952.

Williams, Oscar, Ed. *A Little Treasury of British Poetry.* New York: Charles Scribner's Sons, 1951.

Made in the USA